William F. (William Freeman) Fox

The Adirondack Black Spruce

William F. (William Freeman) Fox

The Adirondack Black Spruce

ISBN/EAN: 9783337177317

Printed in Europe, USA, Canada, Australia, Japan

Cover: Foto ©ninafisch / pixelio.de

More available books at **www.hansebooks.com**

The Forest Commission, State of New York.

THE

ADIRONDACK BLACK SPRUCE.

BY

WILLIAM F. FOX,

Superintendent State Forests.

FROM THE ANNUAL REPORT OF THE FOREST COMMISSION FOR 1894.

ALBANY:
JAMES B. LYON, PRINTER.
1895.

PREFACE.

The following article is from a report made to the New York State Forest Commission in 1894. No claim or pretension is made to any original researches of a botanical nature. The report aims rather to furnish information of a general character concerning this, the leading merchantable species in the great forest of Northern New York. At the same time it is hoped that there may be something in these few pages which may be of interest alike to the botanist, forester and lumberman.

WILLIAM F. FOX.

ALBANY, N. Y., *January* 15, 1895.

The Adirondack Black Spruce.

PICEA NIGRA, Link.

Black, Double, or Red Spruce.

Fr., *Epinette noire;** Ger., *Schwartztanne;* Sp., *Abeto negro.*

Leaves dark green, needle-shaped, four-sided, about one-half inch in length, and set thickly on all sides of the branches; flowers in May, the cells of the antlers opening lengthwise. Nodding cones, persistent for several years, from one to one and one-half inches long, ovate in shape, recurved, with thin, rigid scales having a characteristic broken or slightly jagged edge, the cones hanging on the end of short branches. Bark thin, of a dark-brown color somewhat tinged with gray, covered with roundish scales.

While the principal habitat of this species is to be found in New York, Vermont, New Hampshire, Maine and Canada, it extends northward to Hudson Bay, and southward as far as North Carolina, although it grows but sparsely in Pennsylvania. It is found also as far west as Wisconsin. Years ago it formed a large part of the forest which covered the Catskill mountains, but was rarely found in the western part of this State.

In New York it attains a common height of 80 feet (24.38 m.), with a common diameter of 18 inches (45.7 cm.); and a maximum height of 105 feet (32 m.), with a maximum diameter of 36 inches (91.4 cm.). It prefers a hilly and mountainous region with an altitude ranging from 1,200 to 1,800 feet, and while it is found at its best on mountain slopes it grows readily in low, swampy valleys.

It furnishes a light softwood of medium strength, with a straight close grain. The heartwood has a tinge of red; it is very often white. The sapwood, which is generally of a lighter shade, or a pure white, is about two inches deep in trees which have attained a diameter of 20 inches or more. The smaller trees have a thicker sap proportionately. It has a specific gravity of 0.534; percentage of ash, 0.27; average tensile strength,

---

* The French Canadians call it *Epinette a la bière.*

10,000 pounds to the square inch. It weighs about 28 pounds to the cubic foot, and when perfectly dry, 25 pounds. Spruce pulpwood cut on high land, partly seasoned, will weigh about 3,800 pounds per cord; that cut on low or swampy land about 4,200 pounds.

It is the leading merchantable species of the New York forests, the white pine having, substantially, been removed many years ago. In 1893 the total product of all the mills which obtained their stock of logs from the Adirondack forests was as follows:

	Feet.
Spruce	241,581,824
Hemlock	77,910,654
Pine	27,844,222
Hardwood	7,713,828
Total	355,050,528

The production was still greater in 1892, owing to the low water during the previous year; but the figures given here for 1893 will fairly represent the average annual product of this region. In addition to the 241,581,824 feet of spruce sawed in 1893, the pulp mills consumed in that year 92,135,707 feet, B. M., all of which was used in the manufacture of paper.

Spruce lumber is used for various purposes, but principally for house building, a large amount of it being made into flooring and ceiling, for which use it takes the place largely of white pine. A large share of the product is also sawed into joists, scantling, square timber and dimension stuff. In market value it is cheaper than white pine, but dearer than hemlock. The value of the logs in the tree, or "stumpage," is about 35 cents per market log, or $1.75 per 1,000 feet, the price varying somewhat more or less in proportion as the timber is accessible or within hauling distance of streams which will permit the floating or "driving" of logs to the mills. The value of the logs when delivered on the banks of these streams is about $1.30 per market, or $6.50 per 1,000 feet. The bark has no commercial value. It is peeled from standing trees, occasionally by woodmen, guides or sportsmen, who use it for covering the roof or sides of their shanties.

In the Albany lumber market the log run brings about $14 per 1,000 feet. There is very little clear stuff to be sorted out; a small percentage of clear inch, however, is generally selected which sells for $23 per 1,000 feet. For this market it is sawed largely into nine inch boards, and into two-inch planks, nine inches wide; also into 2 by 10-inch planks. Shingles made from spruce are of inferior quality, and not durable; hence it is seldom used for this purpose. The wood decays rapidly when exposed to the weather, but when protected it will compare favorably with other softwoods in durability. The trees of this species growing in a dense forest furnish tall tapering trunks, free from branches, with an elastic, straight-grained timber, which makes it very desirable for spars and piles. One firm of lumbermen in the Adirondack region ships annually a large quantity of this timber "in the round," the full length of the tree, for this purpose. It is used in boat building, the base of the tree and principal roots furnishing knees, while the best quality of the straight-grained planks taken from the butt logs are manufactured into oars. In the southern part of the Adirondack forest the best trees are selected, from which the clear butt logs are taken for the manufacture of sounding boards for pianos. Only choice logs are used for this purpose, and these are "quarter sawed" into boards five-eighths of an inch thick. This class of lumber is worth $35 per 1,000 feet at the mills. The logs cut for this purpose are known in the trade as "fiddle butts."

Mention should be made here, also, of the resinous gum which exudes from the tree trunks of this species, and which, after undergoing a slight preparation, is sold for chewing gum. A large number of men known as gum pickers follow this industry during the winter months, obtaining a good livelihood from this peculiar work. Years ago a favorite drink known as spruce beer was made by boiling the young branches and evaporating the infusion, but its place as a beverage has been so largely taken by other drinks that now one seldom sees or hears of the old-fashioned "spruce beer." This decoction of the spruce twigs has valuable medicinal properties, and is a well-known antidote to the form of scurvy prevalent among seamen while on long voyages.

The wood furnishes an inferior quality of fuel, giving out little heat comparatively, and, owing to the air contained in it, causing a continual snapping, which makes it dangerous when burned in open fire-places.

Occasionally, this species grows thickly in masses, or what the lumbermen term "clumps," but, as a general thing, it is distributed quite evenly through the forests in which it is found. Throughout the Adirondack woods it forms on an average from 10 to 15 per cent of the timber. The Adirondack forests, as a whole, are composed principally of hardwoods, the deciduous trees including about 70 per cent., among which the remaining 30 per cent. of conifers are, as a general thing, somewhat evenly distributed. The black spruce is here found in company with the maple, beech, and yellow birch, among which there is a further but small admixture of ash, cherry, elm, basswood, and ironwood. The conifers associated with the spruce are composed of hemlock, balsam (*Abies balsamea*), tamarack and white cedar, the various species of pine having been nearly all removed by the lumbermen years ago. Michaux makes the statement that this species "often constitutes a third part of the forests by which they are uninterruptedly covered." One of our leading text-books on botany states that "dark-mountain forests are often wholly composed of it." While this statement may possibly be true of other localities, there is certainly no such composition in the Adirondack forests, aside from the occasional but small clumps of spruce previously referred to.

In some localities there are large areas along the mountain slopes covered with a heavy proportion of evergreens whose sombre hues might give rise to such an impression to a distant spectator, but a closer examination of such forests discloses a large admixture of other conifers, together with a good proportion of broad-leafed trees which are apparent only in summer, and which even then are liable to be overshadowed and hidden by the overtopping or dominant crowns of tall conifers.

In its habit the black spruce has very little of attraction or beauty in its appearance. When growing in masses, all its branches fall off, leaving groups of columnar, tapering shafts, each of which is surmounted by a small, sparsely-limbed and irregular crown; and this is also the case, to a considerable extent, where it is distributed among the hardwoods with plenty of surrounding space. When growing in openings, well removed

G. H. Rison, Photo

BLACK SPRUCE.

Habit when grown in the Forest.

G. H. Rison, Photo.

BLACK SPRUCE.

Habit when grown in the open.

from other trees, its branches are persistent and cover the trunk from the ground to the crown, forming a pyramidal-shaped tree with a conical head whose regular and symmetrical outlines elicit praise from some, while the primness and exactness of shape is objectionable to others.

In growing it attains height by the annual increase of one leading terminal shoot, which adds to its height 10 to 15 inches each year. From the base of this terminal shoot there is formed each year a whorl of branches which gradually shorten in passing from the lower to the upper ones, the lower ones having each one more year of growth than the one above it. The branches, which are in whorls of four or more, are horizontal with a slight tendency to an upward direction. As the trees increase in age the whorls become less distinct, owing to the decay and falling off of the branches.

The black spruce derives its name from the very dark hue of its foliage which, when massed on some mountain slope, is of such a sombre color that it appears to be black rather than green. The name is also used in distinction from the white spruce, whose leaves are of a pale or glaucous hue. In many of our manuals the black and white spruce are designated respectively as the double and single spruce, but the reason for this peculiar distinction is not readily apparent.

These two species bear such a resemblance that it is not always easy to identify them, the cones, which differ but slightly in size and shape, furnishing the principal distinctive feature when the flowering season has past. The white spruce is far less abundant throughout the Adirondacks, being rarely seen outside of Essex county. It is a much smaller tree, and its branches are more persistent, most of the trees being covered with limbs from the pyramidal apex down to the ground. The difference between these species is best described by Mr. Charles H. Peck, State Botanist, who in referring to their resemblance says:

"The resemblance between the white spruce and some forms of the black spruce is so close that it is not always easy for an unskilled person to separate them. The descriptions of these trees, as given in the manual, indicate but a part of their distinctive features, and the characters there ascribed to the edges of the cone scales do not in all cases hold good. Having compared these trees at flowering time the following characters seem to me to be the most available ones for distinguishing them.

White Spruce.	Black Spruce.
Young branchlets glabrous. Leaves six to eight lines long. Cones oblong or cylindrical, deciduous before next flowering time. Sterile aments pale, supported on slender whitish pedicels exserted from the basal cup of scales. Fertile aments eight to ten lines long. Young leaves visible at flowering time.	Young branchlets pubescent. Leaves four to seven lines long. Cones ovate or oblong, still on the tree at next flowering time. Sterile aments tinged with red, sessile in the basal cup of scales. Fertile aments five to six lines long. Young leaves not yet visible at flowering time.

"These trees are in flower at the same time in the same locality. They were in bloom the past season in the vicinity of Elizabethtown the last week in May."

The white spruce of the Adirondacks seems to be an inferior type of its kind. Prof. Charles S. Sargent, in his "Report on the Forests of North America," tenth United States census, in describing this species says:

"A tree 15 to 50 meters in height, with a trunk 0.60 to 0.90 meter in diameter; low, rather wet soil, borders of ponds and swamps; most common north of the boundary of the United States, and reaching its greatest development along the streams and lakes of the Flathead region of northern Montana, at an elevation of 2,500 to 3,500 feet; the most important timber tree of the American subarctic forests north of the sixtieth degree of latitude, here more generally multiplied and of larger size than the allied *P. Nigra* with which it is associated."

There is also a tree known as the red spruce which is occasionally found in the Adirondacks, but more plentifully in Canada. At one time this tree was described as a distinct species (*Abies rubra*), but latterly it is held to be a variety of the black spruce. It has larger cones, and a reddish, softer wood, the latter feature being attributed by Michaux to some influence of the soil.

Prof. N. L. Britton, of the Department of Botany, Columbia College, in an article on "New or Noteworthy North American Phanerogams"* says:

"I have lately been much interested in the spruces, and have observed them closely on the Blue Ridge in southwestern Virginia, where I became familiar with two species, one of which I supposed to be the white spruce, *Picea Canadensis*. The same two species occur on the slopes of Mounts Marcy and McIntyre, in the Adirondacks, but neither of them is *P. Canadensis*, which species I did not see. It is reported from northern New York, but I did not encounter it.

* Bulletin of the Torrey Botanical Club, Vol. 21, No. 1, Jan., 1891.

Fig. 1. Cone and leaves natural size.
Fig. 2, A seed.

From Michaux' N. American Sylva

Black Spruce
Picea nigra

Albany Eng. Co.

Fig. 1, Cone and leaves, natural size.
Fig. 2, A seed.

From Michaux
N. American Sylva

Albany Eng

White Spruce
Picea alba.

"The two species of the Blue Ridge and the Central Adirondacks are the black spruce, *P. Mariana*, and the red spruce, *P. rubra*. By most recent authors the latter has been regarded as a variety of the former, but this view has been ably attacked by Prof. George Lawson in a paper on 'Remarks on the Distinctive Characters of the Canadian Spruces,' published, I think, in 1888. He there maintains that the red spruce is distinct from the black, and I am in entire accord with this opinion. The white spruce is very different from either of the others by its elongated cones, entirely glabrous and glaucous twigs and sterigmata, and very light-green leaves. *P. rubra* differs from *P. Mariana* by its very slender twigs, which are sparingly pubescent, the sterigmata nearly or quite glabrous, its very slender light-green, nearly straight, very acute leaves, and its oblong cones, which are deciduous at the end of the season, the scales lacerated or two-lobed. *P. Mariana* has stout, very pubescent twigs and sterigmata, stout and thick, merely mucronate, dark-green, incurved leaves, and ovate, larger cones, which are persistent for two or more years, their scales entirely or merely erose. *P. rubra*, according to my observations, reaches a much greater altitude on McIntyre than does *P. Mariana*, and this agrees with our collections in the Blue Ridge of Virginia. The very slender twigs of *P. rubra* and its light-green leaves give it a much more graceful aspect than is exhibited by *P. Mariana*."

A noticeable peculiarity of the Adirondack spruce is the large number of defective trees scattered through the forest, which are known as "seamy trees," this defect or "seam" rendering them unfit for lumber. The seam appears to be a crack which extends up and down the trunk, varying in length and extending in some cases from the butt log to the lower branches of the crown. These openings vary in depth, but sometimes the crack reaches to the heart. The edges of the seam are thickly coated with the resinous substance known as spruce gum, which exudes and then hardens, the larger and cleaner masses being gathered by the "gum pickers" who earn a livelihood by this work. The seams are mostly perpendicular, but in trees where the grain of the wood is not straight, the seam winds upward obliquely as it follows the grain. The cause of this defect has never been satisfactorily explained, although various reasons have been suggested.

These seamy trees are not as observable now as before the great blight which, within the last 20 years, destroyed a large proportion of the spruce throughout the Adirondack forests. The seams were confined mostly to mature trees, as the blight seldom attacked trees under 12 inches in diameter. The younger spruces which were spared, and which form a large part of the forest to-day, afford now comparatively few specimens of seamy timber.

About 25 years ago, the black spruce throughout the great forest of northern New York began to show signs of blight, the first appearance of which was noticed in 1868. During the next 10 years this blight spread through most of the forest, only a few localities remaining untouched. Competent authorities who had made a study of the matter on the ground, estimated that at one time one-third to one-half of the matured spruce in the Adirondack region was dead. In some townships there was a recurrence of the evil after an interval of 25 years, the time of the first appearance being fixed by some observers at a date earlier than 1868.

When the trees were first attacked by this scourge, the leaves commenced falling while they were yet green. The foliage remaining on the tree soon turned to a reddish-brown, whose hues made the mountain slopes and forest areas of the valleys appear as if a scorching fire had swept over them. About 1884 there was a noticeable cessation in this destruction of timber, and since that time there has been no recurrence of the evil. The dead trees have mostly fallen, although here and there some tall "stubs" remain as reminders of the calamity. The young trees, which everywhere escaped, now display their green foliage where the brown dead leaves of the blasted spruces were seen, and but little evidence remains of the blight that wrought such a widespread destruction in this class of property.

The cause of this decay or death of the spruce has been the subject of much discussion, various reasons for it having been advanced. Some — among them, men who had been close observers of the blight from its beginning — attributed the death of the trees to drought; but this reason was hardly satisfactory, because the disease killed the timber growing in damp, moist places and swamps, as well as in localities where drought might have affected them; also, on northern as well as on southern slopes. Moreover the alleged drought did not affect in any way the other species, both deciduous and coniferous, which were growing in company with the diseased spruces.

G. H. Rison, Photo

BRANCH OF THE BLACK SPRUCE

Not quite natural size.

G. H. Rison, Photo

BRANCH OF THE BLACK SPRUCE.

One-third natural size.

Some claimed that this premature decay was due to the agitation of the trees by high winds, but the blight attacked also the timber standing in sheltered and protected situations.

It was suggested that the evil might have been due to a hard winter, to some period of intense cold, or to some late and severe frost occurring after the sap had started in its vernal flow; but there is no record of any such unusual weather, and no reason why all the other species, some of them closely allied to the spruce, should not have been injured by the same cause.

Others, including dendrologists as well as woodsmen, held stoutly to the theory that the spruce was a short-lived species, and that the trees died of old age. There was some ground for this theory in the fact that the smaller trees — those under 12 inches in diameter or thereabouts — were uninjured. But, in reply, it has been shown that the spruce is not a short-lived tree; that it is a hardy species which resists the extremes of altitude and latitude; that, where it grows subject to natural forest conditions, it is the slowest in growth of all the native trees of our State, and that there are live spruces standing in the Adirondacks which are nearly four centuries old. Spruces of equal diameters often vary 100 years in age, owing to difference in environment. But these trees died in masses or clumps, the same as when scattered, irrespective of the fact that, though of equal size, they differed a century or more in age. If the trees which died had all been planted at the same time, were all of the same size, diameter and age, and, furthermore, the limit of maturity had been ascertained and determined, then the theory of death from old age might be entertained.

In view of the prevalence of insect blight elsewhere it seems strange that this cause should have been overlooked or summarily dismissed without consideration. Some investigators asserted that they had looked carefully for insects, both on the leaves and under the bark, and failed to find any. This proves nothing, however; the entomologists found them when they took up the investigation.

From statements made by Mr. Peck, the State Botanist, who first discovered the insect at work, and reports of entomologists whose observations justify his conclusions, there seems to be good ground for attributing the death of the Adirondack spruces to the work of a small beetle known as the *Hylurgus rufipennis*, Kirby. Mr. Peck found both the mature insect and its larvæ in countless numbers under the bark of the diseased trees. These insects excavate a passage between the bark and the wood, eating away a part of both, and thus, practically, girdling the tree, their numerous galleries forming an intricate network of furrows which traverse the most vital part. Woodsmen are apt to claim that worms or insects are found only in dead or fallen timber, and entomologists have often expressed a doubt as to any borer attacking a live tree. But both Mr. Peck and Dr. Packard, in their investigations of the Adirondack spruce blight, found these beetles in live spruces, trees in which the wood was full of sap and on which the leaves were fresh and green.

Mr. Peck mentions having found dead beetles in a 10-inch tree. In this case the insects had commenced work, but the resin — which is so plentiful in the young spruces — oozed from the wounds, obstructing their passage, and the insects becoming embedded in gum were found dead, each in its furrow. The older and larger trees having less resinous matter, offered no such obstruction, which may account for the fact that only the mature trees perished — a much more plausible theory than the one of old age.

The reason for the sudden cessation of the blight has been a subject of discussion as well as the origin. The complete disappearance of these insects has been attributed, with good reason, to the woodpeckers, which were observed at work in many places, the dead trees having been pecked at by these birds in search of insect food until the bark had turned to a reddish hue.

It is not at all improbable that there may be a recurrence of this blight, and another wholesale destruction of merchantable timber from this cause. If so, the timber as fast as it is attacked should be cut and marketed instead of allowing it to be wasted and lost. Unfortunately the State law will not permit any such economic action. The sale of any timber in the Forest Preserve, not only the matured but the dead and fallen trees as well, is specifically prohibited. Neither can the law be repealed or amended, for the persons who are responsible for this remarkable legislation succeeded in having it incorporated in the Constitution itself.

G. H. Rison, Photo.

BARK ON BLACK SPRUCE.

Tree 12 inches in diameter.

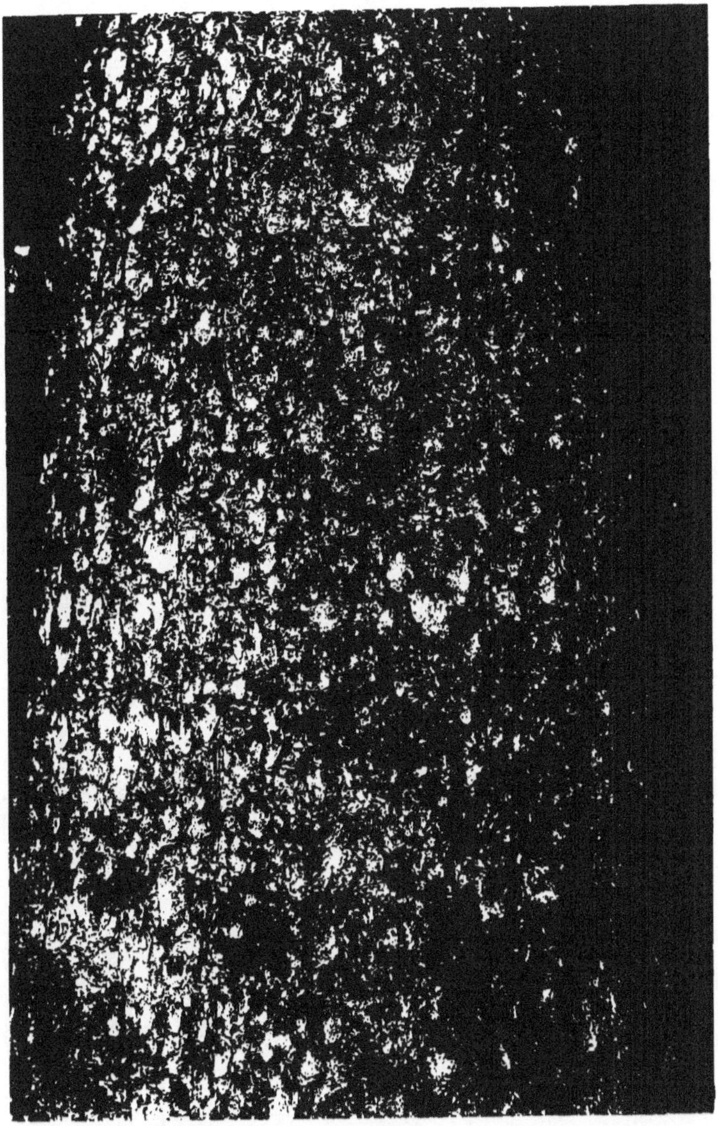

G. H. Rison, Photo

BARK ON BLACK SPRUCE.

Tree 23 inches in diameter.

NOTE.—Unlike many other species the bark on the large, old trees undergoes little change, and retians its characteristic appearance.

Since the organization of the Forest Commission, 10 years ago, not a tree has been cut on State land with the consent of the Commission, and, under the new Constitution, 20 years must elapse before any such permission can be given. But on the lands owned by the clubs or used as private preserves, which include one-third of the Adirondack forest, timber cutting for revenue and also for forest improvement will always be carried on. Where the cutting is done with reference primarily to forest improvement, the trees are taken irrespective of size or species; but where the thinning is done with reference to forest revenue rather than improvement, the cutting will probably be confined to one or two merchantable species, with some further restrictions to prevent the cutting of small trees or those which have not attained a mature size.

Except in a few localities the hardwood timber, which constitutes over 70 per cent. of the average forest, is not cut, while from the remaining evergreens only two* species are taken to any extent. There is little or no white pine left in northern New York. Hemlock is valuable only for its bark, owing to the low market price for that kind of lumber, and is not cut for bark except where there is a short haul or easy shipment to some tannery. Balsam, cedar, and tamarack have so small a place in the lumber market that these species are seldom removed. But the black spruce, which forms from 5 to 10 per cent. of our northern forests is a merchantable species in great demand, and forest owners desirous of obtaining a revenue from their property can take the matured trees of this species without any serious injury to existing conditions. In fact, so few spruce trees are cut to the acre on a well-managed job that their absence would be noticed only by those familiar with the business, there being no apparent diminution in the density of the forest or quantity of foliage. Of course, such a system, however closely restricted, would not fill the requirements for forest improvement; but it does not necessarily imply forest injury, much less forest destruction, as recently claimed by some very good but very stupid people.

Laying aside the question of cutting timber with reference to forest improvement, the cutting on the private preserves of

* Spruce and hemlock.

matured spruce for revenue only, still involves a discussion of certain points closely connected with forestry principles.

No matter how well our people may become educated in the tenets of scientific forestry, or how amply provided our land-owners may be with skillful, professional foresters, the system under which the Adirondack forest must be managed for years, well or poorly, will be the one known as that of "selection." This is indicated by various conditions. Our forests are already grown, and the market price of their product will not warrant anything in the line of planted forests other than some experimental work. Moreover, as only one merchantable species is accessible, the cutting will be limited for a long time to that one species, — the black spruce. In order to insure a future and permanent supply the selection will be further confined to the matured trees, so far as the problem of tree-growth and interest account will permit.

AGE OF THE SPRUCE.

Here arises the question, what constitutes a matured spruce in the Adirondack forests? How old must it be when it grows under natural conditions? How large, how tall, and what must its diameter be? Under any system, whether the thinning be done for improvement or revenue, this point is one of the first to be determined.

For the purpose of obtaining definite information on this subject the Forest Commission instituted some researches, the result of which is here submitted. Acting under definite instructions from the Superintendent some of the foresters, specially detailed for this work, went to different localities in the Adirondack forest, where, by counting the annual rings of tree-growth as revealed by the stumps and cross sections of the trunks, they accumulated a mass of data and statistics which furnish satisfactory information on this point. In counting the rings on the stumps the foresters used large magnifying glasses, which were necessary owing to the slow growth of the spruce and crowded condition of the annual rings. In many cases it would be impossible to count these rings, or "grains" as the woodsmen term them, with the naked eye. The rings were counted on the line of the greatest diameter, and from the center along the longest radiating line. Small pins were inserted at every inch, and the rings in each inch counted and recorded separately. By the latter arrangement the amount of eccentricity in the growth is apparent in each case. In the black spruce the heart is seldom found in the exact center of the tree, this lack of concentricity in the rings of annual growth being a noticeable feature.

The statistics offered first are based on the work done by Forester Humes, in St. Lawrence county, who examined and counted the rings on 237 spruce trees with reference to establishing the facts as to age and maximum size only. The statistics showing number of years for each successive individual inch of diameter, together with amount of eccentricity, are given in other and subsequent tables.

TABLE I.

SPECIMEN NUMBER.	Diameter of stump, in inches.	Number of rings on stump.	*Length of shaft, in feet.	Diameter at top, in inches.	Number of rings at top.	Total height of tree, in feet.
1	30	325	72	11	98	93
2	30	289	68	9	105	87
3	30	315	54	12	123	82
4	30	275	54	11	104	91
5	30	291	58	12	116	92
6	29	333	58	13	112	81
7	29	298	54	10	100	79
8	29	321	54	9	97	75
9	29	287	58	12	103	87
10	29	312	54	14	138	91
11	29	310	54	13	106	83
12	29	273	54	11	94	80
13	28	278	58	10	100	70
14	28	293	58	13	118	76
15	28	273	54	10	84	70
16	28	247	58	8	99	68
17	28	301	60	7	93	72
18	28	300	54	12	68	70
19	28	271	54	10	123	70
20	27	281	58	12	103	68
21	27	302	54	11	98	76
22	27	298	58	10	99	69
23	27	258	54	9	107	80
24	27	259	54	13	156	78
25	27	316	54	10	121	71
26	27	273	58	11	99	81
27	27	301	54	12	136	69
28	27	298	54	14	134	86
29	27	294	58	12	123	80
30	27	284	58	10	118	71
31	27	294	54	14	119	64
32	27	274	54	11	100	80
33	27	278	58	11	87	67
34	27	304	54	11	101	70
35	27	293	58	11	112	71
36	27	278	54	10	97	68
37	27	301	58	10	80	68
38	26	301	54	13	155	84
39	26	302	58	12	102	74
40	26	293	54	12	138	69
41	26	284	54	13	138	80
42	26	354	65	9	102	94
43	26	291	54	12	129	81
44	26	274	54	13	154	83
45	26	271	54	10	98	80
46	26	285	58	13	128	69
47	26	290	54	10	102	78
48	26	258	54	9	100	80
49	26	291	58	12	91	63
50	26	231	54	10	62	70
51	26	261	54	8	92	80
52	26	293	58	12	102	88
53	25	219	44	10	61	71
54	25	291	58	11	100	81

* Not including crown or stump. The stumps average 32 inches in height.

TABLE I — (*Continued*).

SPECIMEN NUMBER.	Diameter of stump, in inches.	Number of rings on stump.	Length of shaft, in feet.	Diameter at top, in inches.	Number of rings at top.	Total height of tree, in feet.
55	25	281	54	11	81	62
56	25	271	54	10	94	80
57	25	219	48	12	99	62
58	25	283	58	10	73	61
59	25	261	54	9	51	73
60	25	300	58	11	91	71
61	25	300	54	11	98	61
62	25	281	57	12	162	71
63	25	300	58	14	152	67
64	25	300	54	11	92	61
65	25	291	54	13	100	62
66	25	195	48	11	76	57
67	25	208	54	8	80	64
68	25	302	58	10	103	71
69	25	271	54	12	94	67
70	25	284	58	13	151	71
71	25	293	54	10	102	71
72	25	273	54	13	103	72
73	25	284	54	9	132	71
74	25	274	58	12	93	61
75	25	281	54	14	152	75
76	25	258	54	11	124	91
77	25	274	58	10	119	82
78	25	271	54	14	120	92
79	25	198	54	10	104	81
80	25	291	56	12	161	91
81	25	267	48	15	126	65
82	24	269	54	14	130	82
83	24	264	54	11	101	71
84	24	274	58	13	121	78
85	24	261	54	11	104	80
86	24	291	58	12	100	69
87	24	272	54	11	93	71
88	24	281	58	12	126	80
89	24	300	62	11	158	86
90	24	271	54	14	132	71
91	24	299	54	13	121	70
92	24	301	58	10	141	80
93	24	291	54	14	132	65
94	24	254	54	11	91	71
95	24	239	54	13	106	61
96	24	267	56	14	123	74
97	24	281	58	12	85	80
98	24	178	54	15	74	68
99	24	267	54	11	124	71
100	24	271	58	13	100	69
101	23	256	54	12	92	67
102	23	300	48	12	120	70
103	23	278	54	11	100	78
104	23	283	55	12	98	71
105	23	291	54	14	141	70
106	23	283	48	11	104	80
107	23	283	58	11	106	78
108	23	300	52	15	151	80

TABLE I — (*Continued*).

SPECIMEN NUMBER.	Diameter of stump, in inches.	Number of rings on stump.	Length of shaft, in feet.	Diameter at top, in inches.	Number of rings at top.	Total height of tree, in feet.
109	23	291	54	12	103	69
110	23	281	58	11	127	70
111	23	271	54	11	97	69
112	23	217	54	14	85	70
113	23	253	54	13	132	71
114	23	219	54	12	116	62
115	23	271	58	11	121	73
116	23	189	48	10	79	62
117	22	314	54	12	155	73
118	22	263	54	12	152	73
119	22	281	54	13	121	80
120	22	283	54	11	82	76
121	22	261	54	10	99	71
122	22	345	58	9	152	69
123	22	204	54	10	91	70
124	22	215	58	8	100	67
125	22	253	54	11	89	70
126	22	251	54	9	93	71
127	22	261	58	7	80	75
128	22	201	48	9	78	60
129	22	281	54	12	121	64
130	22	107	54	9	91	65
131	22	271	54	8	89	71
132	22	201	54	12	101	67
133	22	265	54	7	97	69
134	22	261	58	11	99	72
135	22	198	54	13	75	64
136	21	256	48	9	100	63
137	21	201	54	8	76	61
138	21	251	48	11	103	73
139	21	251	54	11	99	71
140	21	242	54	13	121	74
141	21	201	48	7	100	71
142	21	199	54	10	78	80
143	21	291	54	14	123	76
144	21	271	56	10	99	70
145	21	236	54	12	100	69
146	21	281	54	10	104	76
147	21	261	54	12	123	80
148	21	271	54	8	100	76
149	21	199	54	11	103	71
150	21	283	58	14	99	81
151	20	200	54	11	101	68
152	20	201	48	9	99	67
153	20	261	54	12	89	70
154	20	206	54	10	99	71
155	20	213	48	11	100	69
156	20	204	54	8	87	72
157	20	208	54	7	82	69
158	20	199	48	9	100	70
159	20	189	54	8	100	78
160	20	201	54	11	102	71
161	20	194	52	9	99	70
162	20	204	48	12	132	60

TABLE I—(*Continued*).

SPECIMEN NUMBER.	Diameter of stump, in inches.	Number of rings on stump.	Length of shaft, in feet.	Diameter at top, in inches.	Number of rings at top.	Total height of tree, in feet.
163	20	203	54	10	99	68
164	20	207	54	8	124	71
165	20	289	54	10	124	74
166	19	230	46	11	130	78
167	19	193	54	9	105	70
168	19	208	54	8	99	68
169	19	283	62	7	136	82
170	19	194	54	13	100	70
171	19	209	54	10	100	72
172	19	209	48	8	100	67
173	19	238	54	14	96	72
174	19	189	54	12	121	69
175	19	218	48	9	129	74
176	19	201	54	11	99	67
177	19	231	54	6	76	65
178	19	273	58	10	141	76
179	19	194	54	9	100	70
180	19	201	54	10	99	80
181	19	194	56	12	101	71
182	19	204	54	8	78	67
183	19	207	54	11	121	71
184	19	201	48	12	103	69
185	19	184	54	6	78	67
186	19	200	48	5	100	65
187	19	201	54	9	89	70
188	19	199	54	8	89	71
189	18	183	54	7	101	72
190	18	173	46	9	90	70
191	18	200	54	10	100	71
192	18	179	44	8	92	69
193	17	182	46	6	78	65
194	17	200	54	10	89	65
195	17	156	46	8	100	70
196	17	200	48	7	89	67
197	17	192	50	10	102	71
198	17	172	44	6	78	68
199	16	171	50	5	79	66
200	16	200	54	9	121	73
201	16	178	54	8	79	69
202	16	201	50	11	99	70
203	16	167	44	9	100	62
204	15	178	46	10	97	68
205	15	203	42	9	87	71
206	15	174	48	6	78	63
207	15	183	50	5	100	70
208	14	275	27	11	155	74
209	14	182	48	11	108	68
210	14	156	44	7	89	65
211	14	157	44	7	99	69
212	14	200	54	5	78	64
213	14	145	40	8	88	60
214	14	175	50	9	98	70
215	14	161	48	11	103	67
216	14	182	42	12	99	59

Table I — (*Concluded*).

Specimen Number.	Diameter of stump, in inches.	Number of rings on stump.	Length of shaft, in feet.	Diameter at top, in inches	Number of rings at top.	Total height of tree, in feet.
217	13	176	48	4	35	59
218	13	180	36	6	50	61
219	13	157	42	7	60	57
220	13	150	28	8	76	57
221	13	200	44	10	102	66
222	13	188	40	4	59	58
223	13	162	34	6	87	60
224	13	172	27	8	103	61
225	13	192	38	7	96	70
226	13	200	44	9	136	72

Mr. Humes subsequently forwarded some additional notes which are intended to show the maximum size and age of the spruce. Thus far our foresters have been unable to find any black spruce over 36 inches in diameter on the stump. The stumps average about 30 inches in height, and in measuring standing timber the girth is taken at about the same height. The maximum size of the Adirondack black spruce is indicated in the following figures:

TABLE II.

Specimen Number.	Diameter of stump, in inches	Number of rings on stump.	Length of shaft, in feet.	Diameter at top, in inches.	Number of rings at top.	Total height of tree, in feet.
1	36	350	90	12	102	110
2	36	326	84	8	87	90
3	34	302	86	10	100	93
4	34	374	91	5	67	99
5	34	315	72	11	124	87
6	33	285	68	13	165	89
7	32	280	70	5	80	81
8	31	293	60	14	125	80
9	31	281	73	7	80	82
10	31	276	68	10	100	67
11	31	290	71	9	98	70

Statistics showing the age, size or other characteristics of any particular species should be accompanied by some further information regarding the various kinds of trees which are gro ing on the same ground. To this end Forester Humes, in accordance with instructions from the Superintendent, measured off a tract of four acres, situated in the forest in which he made the measurements and other memoranda embodied in Tables I and II, and noted all the other trees growing there in company with the spruce. These notes are embodied in Table III. This forest is located in the south part of Township 14 ("Bloomfield"), Town of Fine, St. Lawrence county. It stands on the north slope of a hill, the spruce being thickly interspersed with hardwoods — maple, beech, and yellow birch (*Betula lutea*). The land on which the timber stands has an elevation of about 1,800 feet above the sea.

The four acres which furnish the statistics in the following table represent the maximum yield of spruce per acre, the timber being far above the average in size, height and quantity. The spruce on this piece of four acres — not including trees less than twelve inches in diameter — will yield 60,000 feet of logs, or 15,000 feet to the acre. This is a remarkable exhibit; and, in addition to the spruce, the figures indicate 18,000 feet of hemlock on these four acres, or 4,500 feet per acre. The average quantity of spruce per acre throughout the Adirondack forests, on large tracts, is estimated at 3,000 feet per acre, and some townships have yielded as low as 2,500.

Mr. Fremont Fuller, of Duane, Franklin county, N. Y., reports a black spruce, 10 feet 3 inches in circumference, or about 41 inches in diameter, outside the bark, breast high above the ground. This tree, which is sound and healthy, is standing in a clump of spruces with six other large ones near it, and overtops the surrounding forest. It stands on the N. W. ¼ of Township 15, on Lot 3, about two miles from the hotel at Meacham Lake.

[illegible]	[illegible]					
22	7	......	......	1	......	8
23	10	1	3	6	......	20

TABLE I — (*Concluded*).

SPECIMEN NUMBER.	Diameter of stump, in inches.	Number of rings on stump.	Length of shaft, in feet.	Diameter at top, in inches	Number of rings at top.	Total height of tree, in feet.
217	13	176	48	4	35	59
218	13	180	36	6	50	61
219	13	157	42	7	60	57
220	13	150	28	8	76	57
221	13	200	44	10	102	66
222	13	138	40	4	59	58
223	13	162	34	6	87	60
224	13	172	27	8	103	61
225	13	192	38	7	96	70
226	13	200	44	9	136	72

Mr. Humes subsequently forwarded some additional notes which are intended to show the maximum size and age of the spruce. Thus far our foresters have been unable to find any black spruce over 36 inches in diameter on the stump. The stumps average about 30 inches in height, and in measuring standing timber the girth is taken at about the same height. The maximum size of the Adirondack black spruce is indicated in the following figures:

TABLE II.

... regarding the various kinds of trees which are growing on the same ground. To this end Forester Humes, in accordance with instructions from the Superintendent, measured off a tract of four acres, situated in the forest in which he made the measurements and other memoranda embodied in Tables I and II, and noted all the other trees growing there in company with the spruce. These notes are embodied in Table III. This forest is located in the south part of Township 14 ("Bloomfield"), Town of Fine, St. Lawrence county. It stands on the north slope of a hill, the spruce being thickly interspersed with hardwoods — maple, beech, and yellow birch (*Betula lutea*). The land on which the timber stands has an elevation of about 1,800 feet above the sea.

The four acres which furnish the statistics in the following table represent the maximum yield of spruce per acre, the timber being far above the average in size, height and quantity. The spruce on this piece of four acres — not including trees less than twelve inches in diameter — will yield 60,000 feet of logs, or 15,000 feet to the acre. This is a remarkable exhibit; and, in addition to the spruce, the figures indicate 18,000 feet of hemlock on these four acres, or 4,500 feet per acre. The average quantity of spruce per acre throughout the Adirondack forests, on large tracts, is estimated at 3,000 feet per acre, and some townships have yielded as low as 2,500.

TABLE III.

Composition of Forest on Four Acres.

*S. W. ¼, Township 14, Town of Fine, St. Lawrence County.**

DIAMETER — INCHES.	Spruce.	Hemlock.	Maple.	Birch.	Beech.	Total.
9	14	7	6	4	12	43
10	15	......	14	11	8	48
11	5	3	......	3	7	18
12	15	8	12	11	16	62
13	12	5	8	5	17	47
14	14	1	4	6	13	38
15	18	2	5	5	13	43
16	14	7	8	5	11	45
17	14	4	5	10	12	45
18	13	5	3	9	6	36
19	4	3	......	3	9	19
20	4	......	5	6	7	22
21	12	2	5	6	1	26
22	7	......	......	1	......	8
23	10	1	3	6	......	20

TABLE III — (*Continued*).

DIAMETER — INCHES.	Spruce.	Hemlock.	Maple.	Birch.	Beech.	Total.
24	5	2	1	3	......	11
25	4	......	2	......	......	6
26	6	1	......	2	......	9
27	4	......	......	......	......	4
28	6	2	......	......	......	8
29	2	......	......	3	......	5
30	2	......	......	1	......	3
31	......	1	......	......	......	1
32	1	2	......	......	......	3
33	......	......	......	1	......	1
34	......	......	......	......	......	......
35	......	1	......	......	......	1
36	1	1	......	......	......	2
	202	58	81	101	132	574

The average diameters are: Spruce, 17⅛ inches; hemlock, 17 inches; maple, 14⅝ inches; yellow birch, 16⅜ inches, and beech, 14¼ inches. This average does not include trees of less than nine inches in diameter. Number of trees to the acre (nine inches or more in diameter), 144, or less than one to each square rod.*

The statistics in the next following table are based on measurements and counts made by Foresters Olmsted and Sanford, who were instructed to measure and count the rings of tree growth on 1,000 trees. Of this number the first 700 were examined on Lots 33 and 34, Township 20, Town of Santa Clara, Franklin county. This piece of forest is situated about four miles west of the Upper Saranac lake and lies between Floodwood and Long Ponds.

The 203 specimens next following were examined in St. Lawrence county on Lots 34 and 35, Township 3, Town of Hopkinton.

The remaining 97, embracing specimens 903–1,000, were measured and counted on Lots 50 and 63, Township 3, Town of Hopkinton, St. Lawrence county.

Each locality was covered by a virgin forest, the trees examined being the first that had been cut in that vicinity. The

* Not including the young trees under nine inches in diameter, of which there was the usual number intermixed with the undergrowth.

G. H. Rison, Photo.

BLACK SPRUCE FOREST.

Side-hill growth.

foresters were directed to confine their examinations to trees which were 12 inches or more in diameter on the stump, although the lumbermen were cutting the spruce there as low as 10 inches and occasionally smaller. With the exception of the trees under 12 inches in diameter, the foresters examined every spruce stump and top within the area selected until the required number had been measured.

In counting the rings of growth in these trees note was made of the number at each inch of the radius with a view to determining the annual increase in diameter.

In the following tabulation, Table IV, the first column contains the specimen number, the next the diameter inside the bark of the tree on the stump; then follows the number of rings per inch on the stump, counting from the heart outward, and along the line of what might be termed the longest radius; the last or right-hand column on the left-hand page shows the total number of rings, or age of the tree, as indicated at the height of the stump.

On the right-hand page the statistics for each tree are continued, following the same specimen number, which, as before, is found in the first column; the next column shows the diameter of the shaft at the top, or at the small end of the top log; then come the number of rings per inch at the top, counting outward from the heart; the next column shows the height of the stump; the next the combined length of the logs into which the trunk was cut, each log being as a rule 13 feet 4 inches long; the next shows the length of the tree top or "leader" left by the lumbermen, and the last column the total height of the tree as indicated by the combined figures of the three preceding columns.

The short dash or hyphen-mark, which appears occasionally in connection with the last figure in a line, indicates that the radius terminated in a fractional inch and, consequently, a smaller number of rings.

TABLE IV.

SPECIMEN NUMBER.	Diameter of stump.	Measurements on Stump. Number of rings per inch on stump, counting from the heart outward.																	Age in years.
1	1′ 6″	38	8	10	10	12	18	12	18	10	20	16							172
2	1 2	26	22	23	19	19	20	18	10-										157
3	1 2	23	25	18	24	10	16	11	9										136
4	1 1	27	28	16	15	17	20	16											139
5	1 2	28	18	16	15	22	19	19	17										154
6	1 1	28	22	15	7	9	10	11	6-										108
7	1 2	27	23	19	16	13	17	14											129
8	1 3	16	25	20	17	7	8	16	12										121
9	1 5	20	22	30	17	14	12	13	10	7									145
10	1 2	21	29	40	22	10	14	10	9	5-									149
11	1 0	23	22	20	15	13	15	12											120
12	1 0	20	22	20	17	18	16	10											123
13	1 2	21	26	15	21	17	16	12											128
14	1 0	22	26	20	19	24	17												128
15	1 0	27	30	31	18	17	12												135
16	1 1	24	20	22	20	26	22	11-											144
17	1 1	21	23	25	19	17	13	6-											124
18	1 1	28	26	21	22	23	19	10											149
19	1 2	20	21	25	20	19	20	16											141
20	1 1	15	21	26	13	15	14	17											121
21	1 1	13	29	31	26	21	16	7-											143
22	1 1	33	32	25	20	12	10	8	5-										145
23	1 0	30	31	32	25	15	13												146
24	1 2	19	21	25	21	9	9	8	11										123
25	1 2	28	16	18	22	26	26	23	12-										171
26	1 3	26	34	28	23	19	10	15	9	7-									171
27	1 2	26	34	30	18	18	12		10	5-									153
28	1 3	22	24	22	20	16	12	12	17	14	6-								165
29	1 3	17	35	23	21	27	20	16	16	14									189
30	1 2	28	23	22	17	25	25	19	17	21									197
31	1 2	20	24	26	18	13	11	12											124
32	1 4	20	21	30	32	18	9	12	9	6	7								164
33	1 4	19	27	20	25	18	10	8	9	5-									141
34	1 1	28	34	24	27	22	13	10											158
35	1 2	20	25	27	30	20	13	18											153
36	1 1	21	17	21	32	15	13	12											134
37	1 1	25	26	23	18	17	15												124
38	1 2	30	30	29	16	9	10	8	9	5-									146
39	1 0	32	26	26	24	14	15	22											169
40	1 0	36	40	30	17	7	8	7											145
41	1 1	30	30	28	12	11	11	10											132
42	1 0	16	33	23	11	10	9												112
43	1 3	26	28	30	24	14	8	7	7	7									151
44	1 3	26	28	22	22	15	13	12	6-										144
45	1 3	24	23	30	24	15	9	8	8										146
46	1 0	30	25	19	20	17	14	7-											145
47	1 0	28	30	19	20	18	6												131
48	1 2	15	16	24	20	28	25	18	14										160
49	1 2	24	18	18	17	14	13	7-											111
50	1 2	20	23	24	23	21	13	18	10-										152
51	1 1	33	30	24	23	3	13	11-											161
52	1 1	20	8	14	28	30	26	29											174
53	1 5	26	33	30	24	17	8	17	19	18	17								209
54	1 2	32	24	20	21	12	11	18	15										153
55	1 1	30	22	23	27	25	18												145
56	1 0	24	36	26	20	15	12	7-											140
57	1 0	44	50	21	14	13	12												154
58	1 2	46	31	23	26	10	11	12	11										170
59	1 6	23	21	24	25	22	21	17	18	27									198
60	1 7	23	36	35	25	15	9	12	10	11	10	9							200
61	1 0	26	37	23	18	20	22												146
62	1 2	20	33	30	27	20	17	13	6-										166
63	1 1	25	32	30	25	16	11	24											163
64	1 3	34	16	21	15	16	12	15	22										151
65	1 3	31	18	21	16	16	17	20	24	7-									170
66	1 2	20	24	36	18	22	26	23	27										196
67	1 2	30	36	30	25	23	16	16	14										190
68	1 0	25	34	30	20	10	10												129
69	1 2	24	30	26	29	13	16	30											159
70	1 0	25	23	18	14	14	13												112
71	1 2	28	26	25	14	8	10	18	6-										193

TABLE IV.

Specimen number. *Continued.*	Diameter of top in inches.	Top Measurements. Number of rings per inch at top, counting from the heart outward.											Height of stump.	Combined length of logs.	Length of top.	Total height.
1	8½	16	15	11	14	10							2′ 6″	53′ 4″	31′ 0″	87′ 0″
2	11	12	13	15	18	21	10–						3 4	26 8	42 0	72 0
3	10	10	13	26	14	4							3 0	26 8	38 0	67 8
4	9	16	16	19	15	13							2 8	26 8	30 0	59 4
5	10	12	11	15	16	14	6–						2 8	26 8	30 0	59 4
6	9	9	9	9	9	9							2 8	26 8	25 0	54 4
7	8	9	8	7	7	9							3 0	26 8	25 0	55 8
8	11	21	15	8	10	18	11						2 4	26 8	26 0	55 0
9	11	11	13	13	16	13	5						3 1	40 0	32 0	75 1
10	9	14	11	15	13	10							3 0	26 8	30 0	59 8
11	9	13	14	15	26	6–							2 8	26 8	34 0	63 4
12	8	10	13	12	11	5–							2 8	26 8	31 0	60 4
13	9	7	8	13	18	8–							2 9	40 0	26 0	68 9
14	8	18	23	26	30								2 0	26 8	27 0	55 8
15	9	15	16	23	21								2 10	26 8	31 0	60 6
16	10	12	15	18	19	18							3 2	26 8	37 0	66 10
17	10	14	11	12	12	7–							2 6	26 8	33 7	62 9
18	9	11	13	12	12	13	8						3 1	26 8	32 9	62 6
19	9	10	7	13	14	14							3 10	40 0	27 6	71 4
20	8	12	11	13	14	7–							3 4	40 0	29 0	72 4
21	9	13	15	9	11	12							3 1	26 8	31 7	61 4
22	9	14	11	13	13	4							3 2	26 8	33 8	63 6
23	8	11	13	13	14	7–							3 4	26 8	27 0	57 0
24	9	13	14	16	12	12							2 8	26 8	36 6	65 10
25	8	9	13	15	13	8–							3 0	40 0	24 9	67 9
26	9	13	13	12	11								2 8	54 0	30 0	86 8
27	8	14	12	11	11	8–							3 0	40 0	24 9	67 9
28	10	15	12	13	13	14	11						3 0	40 0	21 6	64 6
29	9	13	15	12	13	13							3 1	40 0	27 0	70 1
30	9	13	14	14	12	13							3 0	40 0	24 9	67 9
31	8	12	13	14	12	7–							3 2	26 8	20 0	49 10
32	8	13	14	14	13								3 6	40 0	30 6	74 0
33	9	13	12	14	10	12							3 1	40 0	26 4	69 5
34	9	13	16	11	13								3 0	26 8	34 0	63 8
35	9	16	14	14	12	11							3 2	26 8	33 7	63 5
36	8	14	12	13	10								3 6	26 8	29 0	59 2
37	9	17	14	11	9	13							4 0	26 8	30 6	61 2
38	10	13	13	12	14	11							3 8	40 0	33 0	76 8
39	8	14	14	10	13								3 2	26 8	31 8	61 6
40	8	15	16	11	12								3 0	26 8	30 0	59 8
41	8	11	13	15	18								2 8	26 8	24 4	53 8
42	8	12	10	14	10								2 4	26 8	25 0	54 0
43	8	12	15	14	13								3 2	40 0	30 4	73 6
44	9	13	12	14	14	6–							3 2	40 0	34 5	77 7
45	9	11	13	15	14	8–							3 0	40 0	39 0	82 0
46	8	12	13	14	18								3 1	26 8	36 0	65 9
47	8	13	12	12	16								2 4	26 8	29 6	58 6
48	8	13	13	14	17								3 3	40 0	27 4	70 7
49	10	14	14	15	10	11	12						2 8	26 8	38 0	67 4
50	8	12	14	15	13								3 0	40 0	27 3	70 3
51	8	14	14	15	15								2 11	26 8	24 8	54 3
52	9	11	14	14	12	10							3 4	26 8	24 7	54 7
53	8	16	11	13	15								3 2	40 0	23 6	66 8
54	9	13	14	15	13	13							2 7	40 0	33 6	76 1
55	9	14	14	13	14	15							2 4	26 8	33 0	62 0
56	7	12	14	1[illegible]	12								2 6	26 8	27 0	56 2
57	8	15	13	16	17								3 2	26 8	25 6	55 4
58	8	12	12	13	13								2 8	40 0	21 8	64 4
59	10	15	10	10	14	12	15	18					3 4	53 4	30 4	87 0
60	10	15	12	11	12	10	14	13					3 2	53 4	34 6	91 0
61	8	13	12	13	13								2 4	26 8	24 8	53 8
62	9	15	14	14	12	12							2 4	40 0	35 8	78 0
63	8	16	13	12	14								2 6	40 0	33 7	76 1
64	10	20	15	16	18	12	7–						3 4	40 0	28 8	72 0
65	8	15	14	14	12								3 0	53 4	21 6	77 10
66	8	16	12	4	8–								2 10	53 4	13 0	69 2
67	8	19	16	15	10								2 8	40 0	36 0	78 8
68	8–	16	13	12	13	13							2 0	26 8	30 0	58 8
69	10	18	16	13	15	15							3 8	40 0	32 8	76 4
70	9	15	12	17	19	13							2 4	26 8	40 4	69 4
71	10	17	13	16	16	12							3 2	26 8	32 6	61 4

Table IV — (*Continued*).

Specimen Number.	Diameter of stump.	Measurements on Stump. Number of rings per inch on stump, counting from the heart outward.																	Age in years.
72	1′ 5″	24	24	19	15	12	13	29	8–										144
73	1 4	22	27	33	19	16	21	21	18	14–									191
74	1 5	24	32	35	22	14	15	16	15	21	9–								203
75	1 0	24	23	24	15	14	13	11											124
76	1 1	26	30	22	29	18	20	8	7–										160
77	1 2	29	29	24	25	16	12	11	9	6–									161
78	1 7	20	17	19	18	15	14	22	24	26	6–								181
79	1 5	42	35	25	13	10	7	14	10	13									169
80	2 8	28	20	25	22	14	9	9	10	10	10	9	11	8	14	16	11		226
81	1 5	24	31	30	32	16	14	9	12	15	29								212
82	1 6	28	31	25	21	21	18	16	16	19	8–								203
83	2 8	34	25	18	7	8	20	11	6	10	8	16	14	16	24				217
84	1 4	30	28	27	18	16	14	18	22										173
85	1 6	32	25	32	26	21	15	5	6	10	9	14	6–						201
86	1 6	21	20	19	18	22	24	21	17	18	13	12							205
87	2 8	21	22	18	20	14	17	12	18	18	17	15	18	18	16				244
88	1 1	26	28	25	14	15	6	12	6–										182
89	1 3	20	34	20	24	25	12	16	15										166
90	1 1	16	28	14	21	24	19	28											150
91	1 2	24	23	19	18	15	14	13	28										154
92	1 0	24	26	27	18	19	16	22											152
93	1 2	17	28	24	22	10	14	10	17	7–									149
94	1 8	24	32	31	17	10	11	9	15	8–									157
95	1 4	15	22	30	28	19	10	10	13	14	15								176
96	1 1	21	19	30	27	20	18	14											159
97	1 1	24	28	26	19	20	30												147
98	1 6	22	24	21	20	10	13	12	12	27									161
99	1 0	18	22	19	21	16	20	11–											129
100	1 6	18	17	15	13	12	13	12	12	11	13	16	14						166
101	1 0	24	20	20	30	29	19												142
102	1 1	23	26	30	21	18	16	14	16										169
103	1 2	22	28	18	13	15	14	18											128
104	1 4	14	24	18	18	16	14	15	18	8									145
105	1 4	18	22	18	14	14	14	14	18	22									154
106	1 0	24	23	23	20	20	17												132
107	1 0	30	23	17	13	19	28												130
108	1 4	24	22	18	14	18	11	17	15										139
109	1 1	28	30	26	27	23	25	15											174
110	1 3	17	24	26	20	30	16	17	23										173
111	1 0	29	21	20	18	18	22	10–											138
112	1 4	18	22	16	17	13	15	8	14	10–									133
113	1 4	22	20	18	20	11	17	15	21										144
114	1 4	31	32	26	18	15	16	15	16										170
115	1 2	29	27	19	18	20	14	15											142
116	1 2	23	24	24	20	14	12	14											131
117	1 2	18	28	21	19	14	16	21											147
118	1 4	23	30	19	22	20	17	22											153
119	1 4	28	20	19	27	24	26	18	20	18									200
120	1 7	27	31	29	28	17	14	8	8	15	11								188
121	1 6	22	20	24	26	24	11	11	12	22									172
122	1 6	22	26	23	18	20	16	16	18	16									175
123	1 2	22	21	23	20	19	18	15	17	13	12								180
124	1 0	28	30	29	20	17	26												150
125	1 1	30	33	28	21	11	20	30											173
126	1 1	21	26	27	22	17	20	15	14	15	11	20							208
127	1 0	24	26	30	14	7	7	8											118
128	1 1	23	26	25	18	14	18	17	19										160
129	1 2	24	20	30	32	17	16	9	11										159
130	1 4	18	24	22	10	14	24	26	25	18	13								194
131	1 0	28	30	20	14	8	13	12	6–										131
132	1 0	30	34	29	23	11	12	11	6–										156
133	1 0	32	29	27	11	14	10	10											133
134	1 4	30	36	26	17	15	9	14	15	12	10								184
135	1 1	30	38	22	22	23	19	8	14	18									194
136	1 1	38	34	19	19	18	18	19											175
137	1 1	35	42	35	38	23	8	13	16										210
138	1 2	24	27	22	16	10	9	8	18	9–									148
139	1 2	20	21	17	18	21	18	12	22										149
140	1 1	24	20	22	15	9	10	16											116
141	1 2	23	27	19	16	13	7	8	14	15									142
142	1 1	30	34	17	29	20	18	19											167

TABLE IV — (*Continued*).

SPECIMEN NUMBER *Continued.*	Diameter of top in inches.	Top Measurements.											Height of stump.		Combined length of logs.		Length of top.		Total height.	
		Number of rings per inch at top, counting from the heart outward.																		
72	11	16	17	19	23	12	9						2'	6"	40'	0"	36'	0"	78'	8"
73	8	14	12	16	19								2	6	40	0	41	6	84	0
74	10	17	18	18	12	14							3	0	40	0	23	6	66	6
75	8	12	14	14	12	7-							2	4	26	8	33	8	62	8
76	9	14	16	16	12	14							2	3	26	8	34	0	62	11
77	11	13	17	15	15	15							3	0	26	8	43	6	73	2
78	8	16	13	17	9								3	1	53	4	23	0	79	5
79	8	19	15	11	12								2	4	40	0	26	4	68	8
80	10	18	13	12	12	14							3	0	66	8	24	8	94	4
81	8	15	14	15	16								2	8	53	4	25	6	81	6
82	10	16	16	15	12	13							2	10	53	4	29	7	85	9
83	8	18	19	10	16								2	8	66	8	15	5	84	9
84	9	16	17	11	10	11							2	4	40	0	34	7	76	11
85	8	13	16	12	14								3	0	53	4	21	5	77	9
86	9	17	19	11	15	12							3	1	53	4	28	4	84	9
87	12	14	16	16	19	20	24						3	2	66	8	23	9	93	7
88	8	13	14	12	9	7-							3	0	26	8	30	0	59	8
89	11	17	19	13	13	12	14	8-					2	10	26	8	33	8	63	2
90	9	18	12	17	17	18							2	9	26	8	37	7	67	0
91	8	16	14	12	16								2	6	40	0	28	4	70	10
92	8	17	14	13	15	10-							3	1	26	8	24	0	53	9
93	8	16	10	14	15								3	4	40	0	27	11	71	3
94	9	19	11	12	18	11-							3	1	40	0	31	8	74	9
95	10	17	18	12	13	16							3	0	26	8	34	6	64	2
96	8	19	17	14	19								2	8	40	0	26	8	69	4
97	10	19	19	11	17	12							2	9	26	8	31	5	60	10
98	8-	17	19	15	10	17							2	11	53	4	24	10	81	1
99	8	14	17	14	18								3	0	26	8	23	6	53	2
100	7-	18	16	10	12								3	10	66	8	16	10	87	4
101	8-	18	18	12	15	12							3	2	26	8	36	0	65	10
102	7	19	12	14	10								2	6	40	0	24	7	67	1
103	9	16	21	13	13	16							3	1	26	8	26	9	56	6
104	10-	19	19	12	12	12	16						2	8	30	0	37	0	69	8
105	11	21	9	13	16	16	19	23					3	3	26	8	38	4	68	3
106	8	16	10	14	17								2	10	26	8	27	9	57	3
107	8	19	12	13	14								3	0	40	0	21	7	64	7
108	8	21	16	9	11								2	4	40	0	28	4	70	8
109	8	14	13	17	12								2	8	40	0	20	10	63	6
110	8	15	16	19	10								3	0	53	4	21	8	78	0
111	7	9	14	17	13								2	2	40	0	27	6	69	8
112	7	16	17	12	12								3	2	40	0	24	8	67	10
113	9	21	16	13	12	12							2	0	26	8	39	7	68	3
114	6-	19	18	10	13								3	0	53	4	21	0	77	4
115	8	13	11	15	21								2	4	40	0	27	3	69	7
116	8	14	15	17	12								2	2	40	0	27	8	69	10
117	9	16	12	13	10	15							3	4	40	0	25	0	68	4
118	7-	19	12	16	10								2	7	53	4	19	0	74	11
119	11	10	9	15	15	10	17	16					2	8	26	8	41	6	70	10
120	7	16	20	15	9								2	4	53	4	17	10	73	6
121	5	12	11	16									3	3	53	4	29	0	85	7
122	8-	16	19	13	8	13							3	0	53	4	18	10	75	2
123	9	17	13	14	9	15							2	6	40	0	26	8	69	2
124	9	16	12	14	10	13							3	4	26	8	31	0	61	0
125	9	19	16	12	16	8							3	3	26	8	37	5	67	4
126	11	16	14	10	12	18	16						4	0	40	0	31	8	75	8
127	8	14	17	11	13	7-							3	2	26	8	27	6	57	4
128	8	13	9	19	14	8-							2	10	40	0	26	6	69	4
129	9	16	12	14	18	12							3	0	26	8	36	4	66	0
130	11	15	17	14	16	10	9						3	2	40	0	37	6	80	8
131	9	12	12	17	14	11							3	0	26	8	28	0	57	8
132	8	16	14	15	10								2	10	26	8	27	6	57	0
133	8	13	16	12	14	9-							3	1	26	8	25	10	55	7
134	10	14	12	16	14	14							3	4	40	0	19	0	62	4
135	6	17	10	12	7-								3	1	40	0	18	0	61	1
136	8-	19	16	18	10	12							3	0	40	0	29	6	72	6
137	7-	16	17	15	12								3	4	40	0	23	8	67	0
138	8	15	12	15	21								2	10	40	0	26	7	69	5
139	9	17	14	13	11	9							3	0	40	0	22	4	65	4
140	8	12	14	16	13	7-							2	8	40	0	26	8	69	4
141	9	16	14	14	11	16							2	10	40	0	29	6	72	4
142	8	16	19	14	12	7-							2	10	40	0	30	0	72	10

TABLE IV — (*Continued*).

SPECIMEN NUMBER.	Diameter of stump.	MEASUREMENTS ON STUMP. Number of rings per inch on stump, counting from the heart outward.																	Age in years.
143	1′ 1″	30	34	33	25	18	11	11	9										171
144	1 2	21	35	36	16	9	14	10	10	6–									157
145	1 1	31	30	15	16	15	20	21											161
146	1 0	22	20	29	19	17	15	6–											128
147	1 0	30	28	26	23	17	19	26											168
148	1 0	33	19	14	33	19	16												134
149	1 0	16	17	28	14	18	17	14–											1[illegible]9
150	1 3	24	30	30	21	11	14	15	13–										158
151	1 0	28	27	24	14	7	17	11											126
152	1 0	31	24	23	25	35	18												157
153	1 0	24	23	14	14	10	18	11											114
154	1 2	26	15	12	6	8	10	13	6–										106
155	1 2	24	24	16	11	10	7	7	6	6									111
156	1 2	25	26	30	23	12	12	8	8	5–									148
157	1 1	25	18	22	28	18	17	12											140
158	1 0	25	27	22	17	16	23												130
159	1 0	30	32	31	14	9	9												132
160	1 0	18	16	20	14	12	8	10	6–										104
161	1 1	24	23	19	25	22	7	18	12										150
162	1 7	16	16	18	13	12	13	13	14	11	16	20	14						176
163	1 4	17	17	17	16	12	12	14	9	8	10								182
164	1 1	24	30	26	12	12	13	19	13										149
165	1 1	29	28	24	16	13	9	22	11–										152
166	1 4	24	25	29	16	16	15	17	18										160
167	1 2	21	22	15	14	14	8	16	19										120
168	1 0	23	36	20	22	24	12	19–											126
169	1 2	24	21	22	10	13	12	18	8–										128
170	1 0	32	18	13	14	12	21	8–											118
171	1 0	32	31	26	16	18	9	11											143
172	1 4	23	31	22	15	15	16	17	28										167
173	1 3	28	30	19	27	18	12	18	9	9									170
174	1 5	16	18	20	14	13	11	16	11	16	15								150
175	1 7	18	16	15	22	20	23	14	24	11–									172
176	1 1	24	25	20	21	13	10	17											130
177	1 3	22	24	23	17	7	8	15	7	6									129
178	1 2	18	23	22	18	15	13	7	8	4–									[illegible]
179	1 0	25	18	16	16	19	10	5–											109
180	1 2	20	30	25	20	15	18	12	5–										145
181	1 2	28	21	27	11	15	17	14	7										140
182	1 0	26	23	21	11	12	13	9											114
183	1 0	20	26	17	15	8	9	8											103
184	1 0	20	22	26	17	16	16												117
185	1 1	21	18	17	18	19	11	10											114
186	1 1	16	20	21	14	12	13	11	7	5–									118
187	1 0	17	23	17	15	13	12												96
188	1 0	30	23	21	13	14	13	6–											120
189	1 1	19	20	17	20	8	9	9											102
190	1 1	20	24	17	14	17	12	11											115
191	1 8	24	31	30	18	13	14	8	15	10	20	4							200
192	1 8	31	21	19	16	14	16	17	10	14	10	10							178
193	1 2	21	20	24	23	19	10	12	17	27									182
194	1 0	30	28	23	12	16	21												130
195	1 3	28	21	25	9	13	6	6	18	13									130
196	1 5	22	24	16	14	10	11	9	16	8–									130
197	1 0	18	21	21	16	16	10												108
198	1 0	18	22	30	20	18	20												128
199	1 3	16	17	19	14	18	17	18	9–										123
200	1 1	18	22	21	16	13	11	22											123
201	1 2	18	16	24	18	19	10	14	8										127
202	1 5	22	24	16	14	20	17	13	16	12									154
203	1 0	23	20	22	18	12	20												115
204	1 6	14	18	23	17	15	13	13	15	10	23								158
205	1 1	28	30	23	19	9	11	14	5–										139
206	1 0	26	28	30	21	9	24												138
207	1 1	23	18	21	14	9	14	10											111
208	1 1	24	2	25	24	18	16	18–											146
209	1 2	26	19	20	16	11	17	8											117
210	1 11	20	23	12	17	10	13	10	8	6	9	8	18	10–					163
211	1 6	18	23	16	23	17	8	12	12	14	7–								140
212	1 5	18	26	19	17	14	13	8	11	23									149
213	1 2	18	28	20	21	19	14	12	23										154

TABLE IV — (*Continued*).

SPECIMEN NUMBER *Continued.*	Diameter of top in inches	TOP MEASUREMENTS. Number of rings per inch at top, counting from the heart outward.											Height of stump.	Combined length of logs.	Length of top	Total height.
143	8	14	11	14	16	6–							8′ 0″	40′ 0″	23′ 8″	71′ 8″
144	9	16	16	12	10	15							2 4	26 8	33 4	62 4
145	9–	17	11	14	9	15	11						3 0	26 8	21 6	51 2
146	8	16	12	12	11	10–							3 0	26 8	3 4	61 0
147	6	14	17	12	9–								3 6	40 0	8 8	52 2
148	8	16	16	13	14	7–							2 8	26 8	29 0	58 4
149	8–	16	19	14	14								2 10	26 8	26 6	56 0
150	8	19	14	17	12	8–							2 10	40 0	27 8	70 6
151	8	16	16	16	11	9–							2 8	26 8	25 0	54 4
152	10	27	24	18	15	16	10–						2 8	13 4	26 0	42 0
153	8½	19	18	14	10	13							2 10	26 8	31 8	61 2
154	8	14	14	17	21								2 6	40 0	33 8	76 2
155	9	15	16	8	11	13							2 10	26 8	37 10	67 4
156	8½	16	16	12	12	11							3 1	40 0	24 10	67 11
157	9	17	19	12	10	13							3 3	26 8	40 6	70 5
158	9	13	19	12	12	16							2 10	26 8	34 8	64 2
159	7	16	16	13	11								2 6	26 8	31 0	60 2
160	8	16	12	17	12	8–							3 4	26 8	31 8	61 8
161	7	17	16	10	13								3 1	40 0	20 6	63 7
162	7	19	12	16	16								3 6	56 8	15 0	75 2
163	9	16	16	12	12	12							3 0	40 0	24 6	67 6
164	9	16	19	12	13	8–							2 8	26 8	38 8	68 0
165	7	7	13	16	16								2 6	40 0	25 0	67 6
166	7	13	12	15	15								3 0	53 4	24 6	80 10
167	8	16	15	17	14	11–							2 6	40 0	27 8	70 2
168	9	13	16	16	19	15							2 6	26 8	33 0	62 2
169	9	21	17	17	11	13							2 8	40 0	31 6	74 2
170	8–	16	16	13	13	13							2 4	26 8	35 7	64 7
171	8	18	17	11	11	9–							2 7	26 8	27 10	57 1
172	9	19	19	15	16	8–							3 0	40 0	29 4	72 4
173	8	16	18	18	12	11–							3 5	40 0	26 9	70 2
174	14	11	14	10	13	12	15	12	12				2 11	26 8	42 8	72 3
175	7–	17	11	11	18								2 8	66 8	25 0	94 4
176	9	16	17	18	13	12							2 7	26 8	31 4	60 7
177	10	18	18	18	10	15							2 8	26 8	39 0	68 4
178	7	16	11	14	14								2 9	40 0	21 6	64 3
179	7		15	10	17	12							2 8	26 8	27 3	56 7
180	7	15	14	16	16								2 9	40 0	21 6	64 3
181	8	16	12	11	12								2 11	40 0	12 2	55 1
182	9	19	16	12	14	13							2 7	26 8	30 0	59 3
183	6	11	11	21	14	12							2 10	26 8	32 8	62 2
184	9	16	12	15	11	11							2 7	13 4	36 10	53 9
185	8	12	10	17	14								3 0	26 8	31 4	61 0
186	8	8	13	11	15	10							2 7	26 8	30 8	59 11
187	8	16	14	13	12								3 0	26 8	30 0	59 8
188	8	11	12	16	17								2 6	26 8	26 5	55 7
189	9	12	16	13	14		11						2 7	26 8	34 0	63 3
190	9	13	15	12	11	12							2 8	26 8	36 0	65 4
191	9	17	19	8	14	13							3 4	53 4	26 9	83 5
192	8–	12	16	13	11	14							3 0	53 4	23 10	80 2
193	9	10	14	16	12	12							3 1	40 0	32 10	75 11
194	8–	14	14	13	10	9–							2 6	26 8	29 0	58 2
195	8	16	17	11	9	8–							2 8	40 0	31 0	73 8
196	6	18	13	15	9–								3 1	40 0	22 0	65 1
197	9	20	18	16	11	5–							2 6	26 8	34 0	63 2
198	8	19	19	12	15	7–							2 8	26 8	27 6	56 10
199	6	12	15	15	8–								2 10	53 4	19 0	75 2
200	8	21	16	13	13								3 1	40 0	27 4	70 5
201	8	20	19	16	12	7–							2 11	40 0	23 10	66 9
202	6–	15	14	14	13								3 0	53 4	19 8	76 0
203	7	17	15	9	17								2 2	26 8	25 0	53 10
204	9	21	20	17	12	16							3 3	53 4	27 0	83 7
205	7	19	16	12	12								2 11	40 0	22 4	65 3
206	9	19	18	20	12	15							2 8	16 8	39 0	68 4
207	9	17	18	21	15	16							2 6	26 8	43 2	72 4
208	6–	17	14	15	16								2 10	40 0	19 6	62 4
209	9	19	17	21	12	13							2 11	40 0	24 8	67 7
210	10	20	11	8	7	22	21						3 2	53 4	23 10	80 4
211	9	19	17	16	15	13							3 0	53 4	23 8	80 0
212	9	21	17	12	13	16							3 6	40 0	31 7	75 1
213	9	20	20	12	15	17							3 0	40 0	29 10	72 10

TABLE IV — (*Continued*).

SPECIMEN NUMBER.	Diameter of stump.	MEASUREMENTS ON STUMP. Number of rings per inch on stump, counting from the heart outward.																	Age in years.
214	1′ 2″	26	30	34	23	14	14	8	7-										156
215	1 2	22	16	21	15	13	14	14	12	10									130
216	1 0	14	18	20	19	17	14	9											111
217	1 0	22	21	25	22	17	12												119
218	1 2	28	30	32	26	23	20	13	6-										178
219	1 2	23	20	19	22	20	18	21											143
220	1 0	21	24	22	23	18	19												130
221	1 1	23	19	21	25	12	17	9-											127
222	1 0	26	32	22	27	17	34												158
223	1 6	32	30	20	16	17	15	15	7	22									174
224	1 0	30	32	18	25	18	18	14-											165
225	1 4	28	24	18	27	19	12	14	11	7-									160
226	1 2	19	27	21	24	20	16	18	12										157
227	1 4	22	21	17	11	16	19	13	14	10									143
228	1 4	15	26	21	14	19	20	14	13										142
229	1 4	24	24	17	18	19	10	10	13	10	11								151
230	1 8	23	21	20	17	17	21	22	19	13									173
231	1 8	19	32	28	19	17	13	17	13	16									174
232	1 2	24	32	23	22	26	22	16											165
233	1 8	24	28	19	9	9	18	14	14	20	24								179
234	1 6	30	30	13	16	11	19	22	20	7-									168
235	1 6	28	30	34	24	11	8	13	16	16									180
236	1 6	16	24	14	12	15	11	15	18	27									152
237	1 10	14	18	22	15	10	17	15	17	11	17	12	7-						175
238	1 4	22	25	21	22	16	18	17	25										166
239	1 1	14	14	17	21	19	20	22	30										155
240	1 2	14	23	21	28	25	24	17	17										169
241	1 7	23	20	39	19	13	16	11	13		8	12	20						194
242	1 6	10	24	16	17	17	14	17	21	14									170
243	1 2	40	36	23	23	21	21	17											186
244	1 4	18	30	28	30	17	12	12	11										158
245	1 2	32	21	13	19	15	11	16	11										138
246	1 0	20	24	25	30	20	24	10-											152
247	1 2	19	11	17	23	30	36	12											168
248	1 1	18	18	20	13	15	6	17	36										143
249	1 6	23	30	26	16	17	17	12	16	14									181
250	1 1	17	20	22	20	21	25	20	26										171
251	1 0	26	27	14	14	8	13	10	5-										117
252	1 0	24	19	16	22	24	30	20	25										180
253	1 8	21	25	23	20	23	13	9	13	13	14								173
254	1 4	16	15	14	17	12	19	12	22										183
255	1 6	18	25	24	20	15	13	8	12	12	16								163
256	1 4	32	35	27	25	20	16	7	13										175
257	1 1	26	20	21	19	18	15	16											185
258	1 4	22	28	23	26	18	11	18	14										160
259	1 4	24	26	18	25	16	18	16	17										160
260	1 3	18	16	16	18	15	11	16	14										124
261	1 2	16	16	23	25	21	21	20	10										155
262	1 0	27	19	18	16	16	12	13											121
263	1 0	18	26	22	21	24	18	7-											136
264	1 1	15	18	16	15	12	15	12											103
265	1 2	23	18	15	16	10	10	14	12										121
266	1 0	24	35	11	13	12	14												118
267	1 0	30	32	23	22	17	13												137
268	1 3	26	21	28	20	19	16	22	12										167
269	1 4	22	22	23	18	15	8	16	18	20									162
270	1 5	24	29	20	17	11	14	9	14	13	10								162
271	1 5	21	26	21	22	15	7	6	10	15									143
272	1 2	22	18	16	14	13	14	14	6-										117
273	1 5	22	21	15	13	12	12	10	14	10	7								133
274	1 6	18	18	17	17	18	17	15	10										130
275	1 0	23	31	24	19	15	2												129
276	1 0	18	22	20	16	20	27												123
277	1 4	14	20	17	16	18	15	17	12										129
278	1 4	19	18	17	16	13	20	16	18										137
279	1 2	16	29	23	21	22	19	16											149
280	1 5	26	32	22	34	22	27	20	27	11-									221
281	1 4	28	20	16	20	16	20	18	22	14-									174
282	1 8	22	2	21	20	23	24	18	19	13	13								194
283	1 6	17	19	17	20	9	10	13	23	30	12	26							196
284	1 0	26	20	21	28	25	20	19											160

TABLE IV — (*Continued*).

SPECIMEN NUMBER *Continued.*	Diameter of top in inches.	Top Measurements. Number of rings per inch at top, counting from the heart outward.											Height of stump.	Combined length of logs	Length of top.	Total height.
214.....	9	22	17	17	16	12	....	....	....	....	....	....	2' 6"	40' 0"	30 '6"	78' 0"
215.....	9	21	21	16	16	15	....	....	....	....	....	....	3 0	40 0	33 10	75 10
216.....	8	19	20	17	13	9–	....	....	....	....	....	....	2 8	26 8	37 0	66 4
217.....	8	19	17	19	16	....	....	....	....	....	....	....	3 0	40 0	22 4	65 4
218.....	9	19	19	16	16	10–	....	....	....	....	....	....	2 8	40 0	27 0	69 8
219.....	6–	18	16	12	13	....	....	....	....	....	....	....	3 1	53 4	22 0	78 5
220.....	8	19	19	17	15	6–	....	....	....	....	....	....	3 0	40 0	26 10	69 10
221.....	8	18	19	16	16	10–	....	....	....	....	....	....	2 11	40 0	25 0	67 11
222.....	8	24	21	19	17	....	....	....	....	....	....	....	3 10	26 8	39 4	69 10
223.....	12	24	24	19	19	12	16	....	....	....	....	....	3 2	26 8	40 6	70 4
224.....	6–	16	15	16	14	....	....	....	....	....	....	....	2 8	40 0	19 7	62 3
225.....	9	20	19	18	17	17	....	....	....	....	....	....	3 1	40 0	22 5	65 6
226.....	10	21	2	17	12	13	....	....	....	....	....	....	3 0	40 0	24 0	67 0
227.....	10	23	20	20	16	16	....	....	....	....	....	....	3 6	53 4	25 7	82 5
228.....	9	20	20	17	18	12	....	....	....	....	....	....	3 0	40 0	40 0	83 0
229.....	10	19	19	19	17	14	....	....	....	....	....	....	2 10	40 0	36 10	79 8
230.....	10	2	20	17	17	19	8–	....	....	....	....	....	3 3	53 4	32 8	89 3
231.....	9	19	20	18	17	17	....	....	....	....	....	....	3 4	53 4	26 9	83 5
232.....	9	21	20	20	18	16	....	....	....	....	....	....	3 2	40 0	28 4	71 6
233.....	7	15	18	10	16	....	....	....	....	....	....	....	4 0	53 4	27 4	84 8
234.....	8	18	18	16	14	8–	....	....	....	....	....	....	3 6	53 4	19 3	76 1
235.....	8	20	19	19	22	....	....	....	....	....	....	....	3 4	53 4	22 7	79 3
236.....	10	18	19	17	18	16	....	....	....	....	....	....	3 8	40 0	36 8	80 4
237.....	8	16	17	19	12	....	....	....	....	....	....	....	3 2	66 8	19 6	89 4
238.....	7	16	16	14	17	....	....	....	....	....	....	....	2 10	53 4	23 7	79 9
239.....	9	19	20	12	14	16	....	....	....	....	....	....	3 4	26 8	34 8	64 8
240.....	7	18	17	17	12	....	....	....	....	....	....	....	3 0	40 0	23 7	66 7
241.....	8	16	17	10	18	....	....	....	....	....	....	....	3 1	53 4	21 10	78 3
242.....	8	18	17	16	14	....	....	....	....	....	....	....	2 10	40 0	26 6	69 4
243.....	8	21	19	12	12	10–	....	....	....	....	....	....	2 8	40 0	23 7	66 3
244.....	8	19	20	20	16	8–	....	....	....	....	....	....	2 10	33 8	37 0	73 6
245.....	9	22	13	16	18	12	....	....	....	....	....	....	2 10	40 0	30 2	73 0
246.....	7	18	19	15	16	....	....	....	....	....	....	....	2 6	40 0	21 0	63 6
247.....	8	16	12	23	15	10–	....	....	....	....	....	....	2 6	40 0	27 0	69 6
248.....	8	18	18	10	14	6–	....	....	....	....	....	....	3 0	26 8	24 9	54 5
249.....	8	16	19	19	12	8–	....	....	....	....	....	....	2 11	53 4	25 8	81 11
250.....	9	12	19	16	19	12	....	....	....	....	....	....	2 10	40 0	30 6	73 4
251.....	8	19	12	13	16	7–	....	....	....	....	....	....	2 6	26 8	29 4	58 6
252.....	7	19	16	15	....	10	....	....	....	....	....	....	2 10	40 0	24 7	67 5
253.....	8–	21	20	17	17	12	....	....	....	....	....	....	3 0	66 8	26 10	96 6
254.....	10	22	16	12	19	17	....	....	....	....	....	....	2 10	40 0	34 8	77 6
255.....	10	19	12	22	18	12	....	....	....	....	....	....	2 11	53 4	21 9	78 0
256.....	8	21	16	19	16	9–	....	....	....	....	....	....	2 8	40 0	29 6	72 2
257.....	7	19	18	12	15	....	....	....	....	....	....	....	3 0	53 4	18 4	74 8
258.....	10	18	22	17	12	16	....	....	....	....	....	....	3 0	40 0	26 10	69 10
259.....	10	21	21	14	11	12	....	....	....	....	....	....	3 2	40 0	27 4	70 6
260.....	7	16	19	15	12	....	....	....	....	....	....	....	3 3	53 4	23 0	79 7
261.....	8	19	20	17	12	....	....	....	....	....	....	....	3 0	26 8	30 2	59 10
262.....	8½	17	19	16	16	8–	....	....	....	....	....	....	3 1	26 8	31 0	60 9
263.....	9	21	20	16	14	12	....	....	....	....	....	....	2 11	26 8	29 6	59 1
264.....	10	16	15	19	23	17	....	....	....	....	....	....	3 5	26 8	28 4	58 5
265.....	9	17	14	11	21	21	....	....	....	....	....	....	2 8	40 0	29 7	72 3
266.....	8–	19	19	13	18	11	....	....	....	....	....	....	2 6	26 8	31 4	60 6
267.....	7	18	10	16	21	....	....	....	....	....	....	....	2 8	40 0	21 0	63 8
268.....	10	21	21	19	11	11	6–	....	....	....	....	....	3 0	26 8	29 8	59 4
269.....	8	16	19	19	17	7–	....	....	....	....	....	....	3 0	53 4	27 6	83 10
270.....	10	17	22	17	21	10	....	....	....	....	....	....	3 3	40 0	23 0	66 3
271.....	8	19	19	12	19	....	....	....	....	....	....	....	3 0	53 4	19 8	76 0
272.....	8	19	14	16	17	8–	....	....	....	....	....	....	3 4	53 4	20 6	77 2
273.....	7	16	14	16	19	....	....	....	....	....	....	....	2 8	53 4	21 6	77 6
274.....	7	18	17	16	12	....	....	....	....	....	....	....	3 6	53 4	24 4	81 2
275.....	7	16	17	19	16	....	....	....	....	....	....	....	2 10	26 8	19 6	49 0
276.....	8	19	19	12	17	....	....	....	....	....	....	....	2 8	26 8	22 7	51 11
277.....	8	21	19	11	16	7–	....	....	....	....	....	....	3 2	40 0	24 8	67 10
278.....	8	16	21	21	12	8–	....	....	....	....	....	....	3 0	40 0	21 8	64 8
279.....	8	12	21	13	19	7–	....	....	....	....	....	....	3 2	40 0	22 0	65 2
280.....	10	18	22	17	12	19	....	....	....	....	....	....	3 0	53 4	19 4	75 8
281.....	10	19	19	21	16	13	....	....	....	....	....	....	2 10	40 0	27 6	70 4
282.....	9	16	17	21	13	13	....	....	....	....	....	....	2 6	53 4	22 7	78 5
283.....	11	21	19	19	12	13	16	....	....	....	....	....	2 8	40 0	21 6	64 2
284.....	8	16	19	19	15	6–	....	....	....	....	....	....	2 4	26 8	24 2	53 2

TABLE IV — (*Continued*).

SPECIMEN NUMBER.	Diameter of stump.	MEASUREMENTS ON STUMP. Number of rings per inch on stump, counting from the heart outward.																	Age in years.
285	1′ 8″	25	20	18	19	25	30	20	25										183
286	1 4	24	36	21	15	18	24	18	20	25									201
287	1 0	22	30	26	16	12	11	11											128
288	1 4	22	24	30	22	12	13	20	20	6-									169
289	1 2	26	22	20	16	14	15	24											137
290	1 0	20	18	18	16	18	18	14											122
291	1 5	33	42	21	14	12	14	16	15	14	11								191
292	1 5	29	26	17	14	16	13	6	10	6									137
293	1 0	31	20	22	25	21	16												135
294	1 0	30	16	18	17	14	18												113
295	1 0	32	30	25	19	18	22												146
296	1 1	19	27	17	20	20	18	30											151
297	1 5	20	26	20	16	16	25	24	26	16									189
298	1 2	24	25	34	23	15	17	24	18										186
299	1 0	20	18	10	13	12	14	12	14										113
300	1 0	33	23	22	16	13	7												119
301	1 1	27	16	20	12	17	9	7											108
302	1 2	16	12	13	14	14	15	16	6-										106
303	1 3	16	18	16	16	13	13	14	9										115
304	1 2	21	20	18	17	14	14	15	12										131
305	1 4	18	14	18	13	14	8	9	10	12									116
306	1 4	29	34	19	19	10	18	12	4										145
307	1 1	20	24	22	15	13	11	19											124
308	1 1	17	22	16	21	14	10	19	9										128
309	1 1	22	18	17	9	10	15	12											103
310	1 1	26	30	28	16	21	10	8											1[illegible]9
311	1 1	30	22	34	18	9	20	15											148
312	1 1	[illegible]	26	21	15	7	14	9											114
313	1 0	23	18	15	14	17	15												101
314	1 0	30	24	14	12	15	8	8											111
315	1 2	16	21	20	13	11	11	10	16	10									128
316	2 0	24	26	16	12	10	11	9	10	10	10	15	14	14					181
317	1 5	28	26	24	21	12	7	12	6	8	8								152
318	1 6	19	17	22	18	16	20	21	19	24									176
319	1 6	24	18	13	12	14	13	13	15	18									139
320	1 1	24	22	24	23	12	13	19	9										146
321	1 1	20	18	22	17	11	10	12											110
322	1 0	27	28	22	17	13	14	18											134
323	1 0	24	30	21	14	10	6	7	4-										119
324	1 2	18	26	30	12	11	12	10	20										139
325	1 0	26	32	26	11	10	10	10	8	8-									141
326	1 1	22	24	17	24	20	14	18	24										163
327	1 1	36	33	27	22	25	18	12-											178
328	1 10	18	20	17	13	11	15	13	12	13	14	16							162
329	1 1	24	27	18	13	10	14	10	13										129
330	1 2	28	30	22	17	12	15	14	12										150
331	1 0	22	18	18	15	12	10	8	7										110
332	1 4	24	20	13	18	24	27	23	13										162
333	1 4	21	20	21	17	17	12	24	17										159
334	1 4	22	25	17	15	16	15	18	24										152
335	1 9	21	21	13	14	10	13	8	13	10	15	18							156
336	1 2	24	15	13	16	17	21	18											124
337	1 2	30	20	18	18	14	12	12	9-										133
338	1 8	20	19	17	13	14	13	13	10	12	10	13							154
339	1 4	17	22	18	17	14	20	10	9										127
340	1 2	15	22	18	14	14	18	11											112
341	1 2	24	30	25	26	17	7	12	20										161
342	1 6	24	22	23	27	14	14	11	10	18	7-								174
343	2 0	15	22	18	12	12	12	11	6	7	12	16	10	7-					160
344	1 2	18	24	12	11	15	14	27											121
345	1 5	24	28	28	21	7	12	8	9	16	13								166
346	1 1	30	28	24	9	12	15	22	7-										147
347	1 8	28	17	16	17	18	10	20	19	28	36								211
348	1 10	23	25	30	28	19	15	18	10	17	13	16	10-						224
349	1 10	22	23	24	20	12	13	17	12	12	15	12							181
350	2 0	23	36	35	12	10	13	8	10	7	13	10	15	17	17-				226
351	1 0	30	24	27	24	26	21	33											185
352	1 6	26	31	33	18	12	14	18	8	16	10	5-							193
353	1 0	21	23	12	13	18	23	10-											120
354	1 0	26	25	28	14	20	23	15											151
355	1 2	10	33	20	27	17	13	8	8	9									164

Table IV — (*Continued*).

SPECIMEN NUMBER *Continued.*	Diameter of top in inches.	Top Measurements. Number of rings per inch at top, counting from the heart outward.											Height of stump.	Combined length of logs.	Length of top	Total height.
285.....	8	18	21	17	14	5-	....	....	....	....	....	....	2' 0"	40' 0"	23' 0"	65' 10"
286.....	11	19	20	20	17	18	....	....	....	....	....	....	3 0	40 0	42 3	85 3
287.....	8	14	16	19	19	7-	....	....	....	....	....	....	2 10	26 8	31 2	60 8
288.....	11	21	21	18	14	15	....	....	....	....	....	....	3 1	40 0	29 8	72 9
289.....	10	23	17	15	19	17	....	....	....	....	....	....	2 6	40 0	28 6	71 0
290.....	7	13	19	16	16	....	....	....	....	....	....	....	3 0	26 8	22 5	52 1
291.....	10	17	21	19	17	18	....	....	....	....	....	....	2 4	40 0	32 7	74 11
292.....	8	16	16	20	19	7-	....	....	....	....	....	....	3 0	53 4	22 0	78 4
293.....	7	19	18	17	13	....	....	....	....	....	....	....	2 8	40 0	25 4	68 0
294.....	6	16	14	11	9-	....	....	....	....	....	....	....	3 0	40 0	20 0	63 0
295.....	7	21	21	16	11-	....	....	....	....	....	....	....	3 0	26 8	28 5	58 1
296.....	8	19	16	16	20	7-	....	....	....	....	....	....	2 10	26 8	31 7	61 1
297.....	9	19	19	16	13	15	....	....	....	....	....	....	3 1	40 0	27 6	70 7
298.....	8	20	19	12	12	8-	....	....	....	....	....	....	2 0	40 0	21 6	63 6
299.....	5	16	17	12	.	....	....	....	....	....	....	....	3 2	40 0	21 7	64 9
300.....	6	17	11	16	9-	....	....	....	....	....	....	....	2 8	40 0	19 10	62 6
301.....	7	16	16	17	19	....	....	....	....	....	....	....	2 6	26 8	21 4	50 6
302.....	8	18	18	19	12	7-	....	....	....	....	....	....	3 2	40 0	22 0	65 2
303....	8	19	17	18	4	....	....	....	....	....	....	....	3 0	40 0	26 3	69 3
304.....	7	16	19	17	15	....	....	....	....	....	..	....	3 0	53 4	18 7	74 11
305.....	8	17	17	20	16	9	....	....	....	....	....	....	2 10	40 0	27 5	70 3
306.....	8	18	18	14	19	....	....	....	....	....	....	....	3 1	26 8	32 0	61 9
307.....	7	17	23	15	16	....	....	....	....	....	....	....	2 6	40 0	22 9	65 5
308....	8	19	21	13	17	....	....	....	....	....	....	....	2 8	40 0	24 2	66 10
309.....	8	18	20	16	16	....	....	....	....	....	....	....	3 0	26 8	26 5	56 1
310.....	7	16	20	17	14	....	....	....	....	....	....	....	2 8	40 0	21 6	64 2
311.....	8	22	16	18	17	....	....	....	....	....	....	....	2 8	40 0	25 3	67 11
312.....	8	19	19	20	16	5-	....	....	....	....	....	....	2 4	26 8	23 0	52 0
313.....	9-	16	19	20	16	12	....	....	....	....	....	....	2 10	13 4	44 10	61 0
314.....	9	19	17	12	21	8	....	....	....	....	....	....	2 10	13 4	29 8	45 10
315.....	10	16	20	22	14	9	....	....	....	....	....	....	3 4	26 8	22 6	52 6
316.....	11	23	19	20	13	16	9	....	....	....	....	....	3 1	53 4	18 0	74 5
317.....	10	16	19	12	21	17	....	....	....	....	....	....	2 10	40 0	28 8	71 6
318.....	8	18	12	17	17	....	....	....	....	....	....	....	3 1	53 4	21 10	78 3
319.....	10	19	16	13	20	12	....	....	....	....	....	....	3 0	40 0	24 10	67 10
320.....	9	17	16	21	11	7-	....	....	....	....	....	....	2 0	26 8	28 4	57 0
321.....	10	20	16	17	12	13	....	....	....	....	....	....	2 4	13 4	39 0	54 8
322.....	8	16	19	10	17	....	....	....	....	....	....	....	2 4	26 8	29 7	58 7
323.....	8-	16	21	19	14	10	....	....	....	....	....	....	2 1	13 4	36 0	51 5
324.....	10-	19	20	21	17	12	15	....	....	....	....	....	2 8	40 0	14 8	57 4
325.....	8	16	19	10	16	....	....	....	....	....	....	....	2 4	26 8	19 9	48 9
326.....	9	19	20	18	16	12	....	....	....	....	....	....	2 1	13 4	38 4	53 9
327.....	7	19	18	18	18	....	....	....	....	....	....	....	3 0	40 0	27 0	70 0
328.....	7	16	12	15	13	....	....	....	....	....	....	....	3 4	66 8	12 0	82 0
329.....	8	16	14	14	16	....	....	....	....	....	....	....	2 4	26 8	33 8	62 8
330.....	9	19	18	20	17	14	....	....	....	....	....	....	2 8	26 8	36 4	65 8
331.....	8	16	18	15	13	7-	....	....	....	....	....	....	2 4	40 0	28 0	70 4
332.....	11	19	18	13	17	16	12	....	....	....	....	....	3 1	40 0	30 6	73 7
333.....	7	17	16	15	12	....	....	....	....	....	....	....	2 11	66 8	15 3	84 10
334.....	9	19	19	16	11	14	....	....	....	....	....	....	3 0	40 0	24 8	67 8
335.....	10	19	16	17	14	15	....	....	....	....	....	....	3 2	66 8	25 6	95 4
336.....	8	17	16	15	15	....	....	....	....	....	....	....	2 10	26 8	31 4	60 10
337.....	9	20	18	16	15	12	....	....	....	....	....	....	2 4	40 0	34 7	76 11
338.....	7	17	19	12	13	....	....	....	....	....	....	....	2 4	53 4	25 9	81 5
339.....	8	17	16	19	13	7	....	....	....	....	....	....	2 1	40 0	21 0	63 1
340.....	10	16	19	15	12	12	....	....	....	....	....	....	2 0	26 8	42 8	71 4
341.....	9	18	18	17	15	15	....	....	....	....	....	....	2 8	40 0	33 0	75 8
342.....	8	20	19	16	12	7-	....	....	....	....	....	....	3 4	53 4	18 6	75 2
343.....	10	18	19	12	11	8	6-	....	....	....	....	....	3 0	53 4	28 4	84 8
344.....	8	16	19	11	12	8-	....	....	....	....	....	....	2 10	48 0	23 0	72 10
345.....	9	19	18	17	11	12	....	....	....	....	....	....	3 1	40 0	31 9	74 10
346.....	7	18	19	21	11	....	....	....	....	....	....	....	3 4	40 0	30 0	73 4
347.....	8	17	17	10	19	6-	....	....	....	....	....	....	3 3	66 8	18 6	88 5
348.....	11	7	15	16	21	24	12-	....	....	....	....	....	3 2	53 4	26 7	83 1
349.....	11	16	14	14	19	11	8-	....	....	....	....	....	4 0	53 4	25 4	82 8
350.....	10	11	13	16	18	26	....	....	....	....	....	....	3 10	66 8	22 0	92 6
351.....	8	19	18	15	12	8-	....	....	....	....	....	....	2 4	40 0	27 6	69 10
352.....	9	12	19	16	9	15	....	....	....	....	....	....	1 8	53 4	22 8	77 8
353.....	9	16	17	21	12	12	....	....	....	....	....	....	3 0	26 8	30 7	60 3
354.....	8	18	19	20	13	8-	....	....	....	....	....	....	2 0	26 8	24 0	52 8
355.....	8	16	20	18	14	6-	....	....	....	....	....	....	2 1	40 0	27 6	69 7

Table IV — (*Continued*).

Specimen number.	Diameter of stump.	Measurements on Stump.																	Age in years.
		Number of rings per inch on stump, counting from the heart outward.																	
356.....	1' 2"	26	32	20	17	20	26	18	....	....	....	....	....	....	....	....	....	....	159
357.....	1 4	24	31	13	21	17	14	18	16	6-	....	....	....	....	....	....	....	....	160
358.....	1 6	35	45	24	27	21	13	10	6	10	....	....	....	....	....	....	....	....	191
359.....	1 2	37	37	16	30	28	17	14	....	....	....	....	....	....	....	....	....	....	179
360.....	1 11	21	31	36	20	17	13	8	9	15	20	24	20	....	....	....	....	....	234
361.....	1 0	30	36	32	22	21	15	10	....	....	....	....	....	....	....	....	....	....	166
362.....	1 0	38	31	20	17	13	18	11-	....	....	....	....	....	....	....	....	....	....	148
363.....	1 2	25	23	23	25	24	23	28	17	8-	....	....	....	....	....	....	....	....	196
364.....	1 6	30	38	14	11	10	15	16	18	23	....	....	....	....	....	....	....	....	173
365.....	1 0	16	25	18	20	19	24	8-	....	....	....	....	....	....	....	....	....	....	130
366.....	1 5	35	24	25	28	13	12	8	18	14	....	....	....	....	....	....	....	....	177
367.....	1 4	25	20	21	13	13	12	18	21	....	....	....	....	....	....	....	....	....	146
368.....	1 8	28	30	26	13	13	10	11	12	12	16	13	....	....	....	....	....	....	184
369.....	1 3	15	19	15	16	17	12	18	15	....	....	....	....	....	....	....	....	....	127
370	1 0	30	34	19	18	20	24	....	....	....	....	....	....	....	....	....	....	....	145
371.....	1 8	18	17	17	14	12	9	10	9	14	12	28	....	....	....	....	....	....	158
372.....	1 4	28	25	12	11	9	17	20	23	6-	....	....	....	....	....	....	....	....	151
373.....	1 6	25	22	17	16	13	11	10	8	13	11	6-	....	....	....	....	....	....	152
374.....	1 3	18	27	25	24	15	12	18	11-	....	....	....	....	....	....	....	....	....	150
375.....	1 4	16	17	15	17	23	12	16	17	18	30	....	....	....	....	....	....	....	181
376.....	1 0	20	18	20	17	8	10	9	....	....	....	....	....	....	....	....	....	....	102
377.....	1 0	28	23	20	13	10	9	11	7-	....	....	....	....	....	....	....	....	....	120
378.....	1 4	46	24	20	15	14	16	20	30	....	....	....	....	....	....	....	....	....	185
379.....	1 3	36	14	13	18	22	13	18	19	....	....	....	....	....	....	....	....	....	153
380.....	1 0	13	31	24	38	24	22	....	....	....	....	....	....	....	....	....	....	....	152
381.....	1 5	18	36	23	21	20	7	7	15	10	....	....	....	....	....	....	....	....	157
382.....	1 4	28	26	30	20	12	12	13	28	....	....	....	....	....	....	....	....	....	169
383.....	2 0	19	19	23	15	11	17	10	10	6	11	6	8	11	8	12	10	12-	208
384.....	1 6	19	42	27	11	12	14	10	13	13	22	....	....	....	....	....	....	....	181
385.....	1 4	20	28	32	18	19	16	20	16	....	....	....	....	....	....	....	....	....	169
386.....	1 2	18	25	22	17	9	11	13	....	....	....	....	....	....	....	....	....	....	115
387.....	1 4	23	19	30	35	23	8	9	6	9	11	....	....	....	....	....	....	....	173
388.....	1 0	17	30	20	18	11	20	18	....	....	....	....	....	....	....	....	....	....	134
389.....	1 2	29	21	20	18	22	16	23	12-	....	....	....	....	....	....	....	....	....	164
390.....	1 6	20	19	14	16	16	19	18	9	11	13	8-	....	....	....	....	....	....	167
391....	1 1	30	33	16	25	13	16	8-	....	....	....	....	....	....	....	....	....	....	141
392.....	1 0	36	25	13	15	10	17	....	....	....	....	....	....	....	....	....	....	....	136
393.....	2 0	36	22	17	16	8	9	10	14	30	16	15	26	....	....	....	....	....	219
394.....	1 8	22	27	20	20	12	13	8	9	8	12	18	....	....	....	....	....	....	179
395.....	1 2	19	21	18	16	17	19	10	5-	....	....	....	....	....	....	....	....	....	132
396. ...	1 4	23	27	24	22	18	12	13	22	8-	....	....	....	....	....	....	....	....	169
397.....	1 7	25	21	17	21	13	14	15	17	17	22	....	....	....	....	....	....	....	193
398.....	1 1	24	30	22	18	11	6	13	13	....	....	....	....	....	....	....	....	....	142
399.....	1 1	20	18	27	23	21	17	20	....	....	....	....	....	....	....	....	....	....	151
400.....	2 1	12	22	13	17	25	14	14	14	13	15	16	12	26	....	....	....	....	213
401.....	1 3	31	26	16	14	15	13	11	9	4-	....	....	....	....	....	....	....	....	142
402.....	1 0	21	21	21	17	13	23	9	....	....	....	....	....	....	....	....	....	....	125
403.....	1 4	28	28	21	17	16	13	13	13	....	....	....	....	....	....	....	....	....	149
404.....	1 2	27	45	14	26	17	12	18	21	10-	....	....	....	....	....	....	....	....	186
405.....	1 4	26	28	30	19	16	16	19	20	....	....	....	....	....	....	....	....	....	174
406.....	1 8	22	24	24	15	18	13	12	14	13	12	26	....	....	....	....	....	....	193
407.....	1 5	30	28	11	12	19	22	17	14	27	....	....	....	....	....	....	....	....	183
408.....	1 10	22	24	23	12	13	15	15	14	14	17	28	....	....	....	....	....	....	195
409.....	1 9	36	42	29	11	11	6	11	8	12	18	11	13	19	....	....	....	....	227
410.....	1 8	25	22	31	18	12	13	12	16	20	23	11-	....	....	....	....	....	....	203
411.....	1 7	40	27	27	16	13	14	9	8	10	14	10	....	....	....	....	....	....	187
412.....	1 5	30	26	24	14	13	16	6	15	8	13	....	....	....	....	....	....	....	165
413.....	1 6	26	30	36	15	11	12	14	8	7	15	14	....	....	....	....	....	....	188
414.....	1 1	26	20	23	17	16	8	7	8	....	....	....	....	....	....	....	....	....	124
415.....	1 5	22	18	16	21	12	12	10	9	5-	....	....	....	....	....	....	....	....	125
416.....	1 1	30	34	21	13	12	23	8-	....	....	....	....	....	....	....	....	....	....	141
417.....	1 2	23	18	19	18	17	13	9	9-	....	....	....	....	....	....	....	....	....	126
418.....	1 2	23	26	16	15	15	13	14	11	....	....	....	....	....	....	....	....	....	133
419.....	1 2	24	28	21	20	16	16	10	13	....	....	....	....	....	....	....	....	....	143
420.....	1 5	31	34	27	21	16	18	10	20	18	....	....	....	....	....	....	....	....	198
421.....	1 0	24	34	19	22	17	16	10	10	....	....	....	....	....	....	....	....	....	150
422.....	1 1	24	30	32	30	24	13	7	....	....	....	....	....	....	....	....	....	....	160
423.....	1 0	24	26	20	21	18	14	10	....	....	....	....	....	....	....	....	....	....	133
424.....	1 2	30	30	27	12	15	9	16	13	6-	....	....	....	....	....	....	....	....	158
425.....	1 1	20		23	16	17	10	9	10	....	....	....	....	....	....	....	....	....	105
426.....	1 1	27	26	18	27	15	13	15	....	....	....	....	....	....	....	....	....	....	138

TABLE IV — (*Continued*).

SPECIMEN NUMBER *Continued.*	Diameter of top in inches.	Top Measurements. Number of rings per inch at top, counting from the heart outward.											Height of stump.	Combined length of logs.	Length of top.	Total height.
356.....	8	12	22	21	17	10-							2′ 3″	40′ 0″	24′ 8″	66′ 11″
357.....	8	16	19	20	20								2 0	53 4	26 8	82 0
358.....	8	17	20	18	15	7-							1 8	53 4	19 4	74 4
359.....	8	19	19	12	16	6-							2 0	53 4	24 0	79 4
360.....	10	8	18	20	23	19							2 3	66 8	18 6	87 5
361.....	7-	16	12	9	14								2 0	26 8	27 4	56 0
362.....	8	17	21	23	11								3 0	26 8	25 7	55 3
363.....	8	21	16	12	13	7-							2 8	40 0	35 10	78 6
364.....	11	21	22	17	11	13	9-						2 8	40 0	39 9	82 5
365.....	8	16	9	22	13	7-							2 6	40 0	23 6	66 0
366.....	9	10	16	23	15	12							2 4	53 4	21 0	76 8
367.....	8	12	19	19	16	6-							2 3	53 4	24 8	80 3
368.....	8	17	21	11	18	9-							3 0	53 4	25 6	81 10
369.....	9	19	16	21	[illegible]	12							2 8	26 8	26 0	55 4
370.....	8-	21	11	20	15	10-							2 6	26 8	22 10	52 0
371.....	8	6	12	20	27	11-							3 10	66 8	18 6	89 0
372.....	11	19	22	[illegible]	18	12	11-						2 4	26 8	36 0	65 0
373.....	10	16	20	21	19	14							3 0	40 0	33 10	76 10
374.....	9	9	23	17	12	16							2 10	40 0	22 6	65 4
375.....	8	2	12	19	15								2 8	53 4	22 0	78 0
376.....	8-	16	19	21	12	8-							2 4	13 4	31 6	47 2
377.....	8	17	22	10	12	8-							2 5	26 8	27 5	56 6
378.....	10	23	20	27	14	23							2 0	26 8	37 4	66 0
379.....	8	9	21	19	12	7-							2 8	40 0	22 7	65 3
380.....	8	12	19	26	15								2 10	26 8	20 10	50 4
381.....	8	20	16	19	13								3 0	40 0	18 0	61 0
382.....	9	20	22	15	17	16							3 1	40 0	25 4	68 5
383.....	11	8	12	8	12	16	18	19	20				2 8	40 0	42 6	85 2
384.....	9	16	20	21	8	13							2 4	53 4	28 4	84 0
385.....	7	8	17	22	11								2 8	53 4	20 4	76 4
386.....	8	17	18	20	19	8-							2 3	40 0	33 0	75 3
387.....	8	10	17	13	19	6-							2 6	40 0	15 8	58 2
388.....	9-	9	16	24	18	12							2 2	26 8	30 0	58 10
389.....	7-	7	15	23	21	16							3 6	53 4	12 0	68 10
390.....	10	22	19	12	15	12							3 0	40 0	34 4	77 4
391.....	9	18	21	23	15	9							2 4	26 8	39 0	68 0
392.....	8	18	19	24	12								2 3	26 8	37 6	66 5
393.....	22	21	13	12	14	13	15	13	16	16	22	23	3 2	13 4	75 0	91 6
394.....	9	12	17	23	21	13							2 4	40 0	33 0	75 4
395.....	8	14	16	19	19	16							2 6	26 8	32 4	61 6
396.....	8	10	21	22	12	10-							2 8	53 4	16 6	72 6
397.....	10	15	11	23	19	12							2 9	55 4	24 8	82 9
398.....	9	11	....	21	17	12	9-						2 4	26 8	32 6	61 6
399.....	7-	16	14	19	17								2 8	40 0	30 0	72 8
400.....	14	14	9	10	12	17	12	13	23				2 10	53 4	39 10	96 0
401.....	9	16	21	23	12	12							2 8	40 0	31 0	73 8
402.....	8	18	17	19	20								3 0	26 8	27 6	57 2
403.....	8	12	19	19	21	9-							3 3	40 0	22 8	65 11
404.....	8	17	19	22	13								2 8	40 0	25 0	67 8
405.....	10-	9	16	21	23	19	7-						3 2	40 0	38 4	81 6
406.....	10-	8	12	16	22	23	27						2 10	53 4	25 7	81 9
407.....	9	21	18	12	20	23							2 5	53 4	31 3	87 0
408.....	9-	11	20	21	17	17							2 6	53 4	24 4	80 2
409.....	9	12	17	23	24	9-							2 8	53 4	25 8	81 8
410.....	11	11	20	26	19	12	13						3 0	40 0	40 6	83 6
411.....	9	16	18	21	18	23							2 10	53 4	26 7	82 9
412.....	10	12	20	22	18	16							2 8	40 0	23 4	66 0
413.....	8	16	19	17	22								2 7	53 4	27 0	82 11
414.....	7	10	13	19	14								2 2	40 0	23 7	65 9
415.....	9	18	12	23	19	12							2 2	40 0	32 8	74 10
416.....	7	18	21	13	17								2 6	40 0	28 6	71 0
417.....	8	16	14	19	14								2 5	40 0	26 10	69 3
418.....	9	13	21	23	16	9-							2 4	40 0	26 10	69 2
419.....	8-	16	17	26	17	12							2 6	40 0	32 4	74 10
420.....	9	11	23	26	17	12							2 3	40 0	31 0	73 3
421.....	8	13	19	12	21								2 2	26 8	30 3	59 1
422.....	8	16	9	17	19	6-							2 6	40 0	32 10	75 4
423.....	8	12	21	19	21								3 1	26 8	29 8	59 5
424.....	12	16	23	20	22	24	21						3 10	13 4	52 8	69 10
425.....	8	12	16	18	20								2 10	40 0	22 6	65 4
426.....	8-	17	17	22	14	9-							2 11	26 8	29 6	59 1

TABLE IV — (*Continued*).

Specimen Number.	Diameter of stump.	Measurements on Stump. Number of rings per inch on stump, counting from the heart outward.																	Age in years.
427.....	1′ 0″	18	20	26	28	23	19	....	....	....	....	....	....	....	....	....	....	....	134
428.....	1 2	17	20	17	18	18	11	8	9	5-	....	....	....	....	....	....	....	....	118
429.....	1 0	16	30	36	10	11	13	12	....	....	....	....	....	....	....	....	....	....	128
430.....	1 1	20	23	28	20	17	12	6-	....	....	....	....	....	....	....	....	....	....	126
431.....	1 4	23	17	18	15	8	16	17	13-	..	....	....	....	....	....	....	....	....	129
432.....	1 5	25	13	14	18	16	15	19	11	10	....	....	....	....	....	....	....	....	141
433.....	1 1	22	15	12	17	27	22	16	....	....	....	....	....	....	....	....	....	....	131
434.....	1 2	20	16	13	17	16	11	18	12	....	....	....	....	....	....	....	....	....	123
435.....	1 1	22	17	15	13	15	17	20	7-	....	....	....	....	....	....	....	....	....	126
436.....	1 1	30	20	21	14	14	12	16	20	....	....	....	....	....	....	....	....	....	147
437.....	1 0	14	15	20	24	21	14	....	....	....	....	....	....	....	....	....	....	....	108
438.....	1 0	20	22	14	13	12	22	10-	....	....	....	....	....	....	....	....	....	....	113
439.....	1 6	14	13	16	12	10	11	12	14	12	11	....	....	....	....	....	....	....	130
440.....	1 1	26	20	11	11	16	15	18	....	...	....	....	....	....	....	....	....	....	117
441.....	1 4	14	14	16	16	13	15	16	24	9-	...	....	....	....	....	....	....	....	137
442.....	1 6	19	15	12	14	19	16	15	22	24	11-	....	....	....	....	....	....	....	167
443.....	1 1	30	23	28	14	17	15	18	9-	....	....	....	....	....	....	....	....	...	148
444.....	1 6	19	19	13	15	12	15	16	15	10	16	14	10	....	....	....	....	....	174
445.....	2 0	15	19	13	14	12	14	11	13	11	12	13	10	....	....	....	....	....	163
446.....	1 0	13	19	25	19	22	24	34	....	....	....	....	....	....	....	....	....	....	156
447.....	1 2	13	18	19	14	13	19	28	8-	....	...	....	....	....	....	....	....	....	127
448.....	1 0	14	17	16	14	13	17	10-	....	....	....	....	....	....	....	....	....	....	101
449.....	1 6	20	19	21	28	17	10	16	17	11	13	....	....	....	....	....	....	....	172
450.....	1 2	12	13	17	18	18	15	10	10-	....	....	....	....	....	....	....	....	....	113
451.....	1 6	16	16	20	18	16	14	12	12	20	10-	....	....	....	....	....	....	....	154
452.....	1 0	18	25	23	34	30	28	....	....	....	....	....	....	....	....	....	....	....	158
453.....	1 1	24	22	20	16	22	20	10-	....	....	....	....	....	....	....	....	....	...	134
454.....	1 1	17	17	15	16	15	12	22	....	....	....	....	....	....	....	....	....	....	114
455.....	1 6	13	17	15	13	14	8	9	18	22	18-	....	....	....	....	....	....	....	147
456.....	1 8	16	16	13	11	12	7	10	9	8	11	9	11	....	....	....	....	....	133
457.....	1 4	14	13	11	10	14	15	9	15	23	10-	....	....	....	....	....	....	....	134
458.....	1 0	19	17	24	23	21	15	5-	....	....	....	....	....	....	....	....	....	...	124
459.....	1 3	15	14	15	18	17	18	18	16	7-	....	....	....	....	....	....	....	....	138
460.....	1 4	17	12	13	13	15	13	13	16	23	9-	....	....	....	...	....	....	....	144
461.....	1 4	23	20	15	17	15	15	17	21	19	....	....	....	....	....	....	....	....	162
462.....	1 6	20	16	12	14	8	11	12	16	11	25	8-	....	....	....	....	....	....	153
463.....	1 5	16	13	17	15	12	17	12	22	13	....	....	....	....	....	....	....	....	137
464.....	1 2	19	18	18	20	15	16	17	23	6-	....	....	....	...	....	....	....	...	152
465.....	1 1	20	17	14	19	19	15	9	....	....	....	....	....	....	....	....	....	...	113
466.....	1 2	18	16	17	16	17	18	12	7-	....	....	....	....	....	....	....	....	....	121
467.....	1 4	15	14	14	15	19	12	18	15	12	6-	....	....	....	....	....	....	....	140
468.....	1 5	19	19	16	16	10	9	9	15	22	14	....	....	....	....	....	....	....	149
469.....	1 2	20	15	15	14	14	15	19	12	....	....	....	....	....	....	....	....	....	124
470.....	1 3	20	25	17	10	12	11	15	26	....	....	....	....	....	....	....	....	....	136
471.....	1 4	20	16	17	12	12	10	20	21	14	....	....	....	....	....	....	....	....	142
472.....	1 3	32	22	17	13	11	12	9	8	5-	....	....	....	....	....	....	....	....	129
473.....	1 0	16	20	19	16	18	21	9-	....	....	....	....	....	....	....	....	....	....	119
474.....	1 6	13	36	16	15	10	13	9	18	30	....	....	....	...	....	....	....	....	160
475.....	1 6	14	23	20	14	14	12	11	16	10	11	8-	....	....	....	....	....	....	153
476.....	1 2	22	20	24	22	17	18	19	14	....	....	....	....	....	....	....	....	....	156
477.....	1 0	32	24	16	17	13	14	18	....	....	....	....	....	....	....	....	....	....	134
478.....	1 2	18	22	12	13	10	14	15	....	....	....	....	....	....	...	....	....	....	104
479.....	1 0	23	22	22	27	19	23	....	....	....	....	....	....	....	....	....	....	...	136
480.....	1 2	24	19	15	18	18	16	17	9	7-	....	....	....	....	....	....	....	....	143
481.....	1 2	30	24	16	13	12	11	9	5-	....	....	....	....	....	....	....	....	....	120
482.....	1 0	18	24	17	18	21	22	....	....	....	....	....	....	....	....	....	....	....	120
483.....	1 0	18	21	20	23	18	22	13-	....	....	....	...	....	....	....	....	....	....	135
484.....	1 4	26	24	23	14	12	15	10	16	12	5-	....	....	....	....	....	....	....	157
485.....	1 1	27	18	17	17	17	11	10	....	....	....	....	....	....	....	....	....	....	117
486.....	1 1	18	23	16	14	15	11	10	....	....	....	....	....	....	....	....	....	....	106
487.....	1 2	24	26	16	15	12	11	9	7	10	....	....	....	....	....	....	....	....	130
488.....	1 0	25	20	17	14	14	11	11	....	....	....	....	....	....	....	....	....	....	112
489.....	1 1	33	30	20	12	10	12	12	6-	....	....	....	....	....	....	....	....	....	135
490.....	1 1	27	24	20	15	12	16	19	....	....	....	....	....	....	....	....	....	....	133
491.....	1 0	27	20	16	21	18	16	....	....	....	....	....	....	....	....	....	....	....	123
492.....	1 0	32	30	24	11	16	15	....	....	....	....	....	....	....	....	....	....	....	128
493.....	1 2	29	26	19	16	15	16	15	10	...	....	....	....	....	....	....	....	....	146
494.....	1 8	29	29	13	12	12	13	19	18	....	....	....	....	....	....	....	....	....	145
495.....	1 1	17	20	17	13	13	22	18	....	....	....	....	....	....	....	....	....	....	120
496.....	1 4	26	32	20	17	13	20	14	....	....	....	....	....	....	....	....	....	....	142
497.....	1 1	26	21	21	16	20	22	13	....	....	....	....	....	....	....	....	....	....	139

TABLE IV — (*Continued*).

SPECIMEN NUMBER *Continued.*	Diameter of top in inches.	TOP MEASUREMENTS. Number of rings per inch at top, counting from the heart outward.											Height of stump.	Combined length of logs.	Length of top.	Total height.
427	8	16	19	10	24	....	....	....	....	....	....	....	2' 0"	26' 8"	21' 10"	50' 6"
428	10-	21	23	10	17	12	19	....	....	....	....	....	3 2	26 8	36 8	66 6
429	8	12	16	23	16	....	....	....	....	....	....	....	2 6	26 8	24 4	53 6
430	8	19	11	17	12	9-	....	....	....	....	....	....	3 0	26 8	23 7	53 3
431	8-	12	20	19	10	15	....	....	....	....	....	....	3 10	40 0	30 0	73 10
432	10	17	22	20	11	18	....	....	....	....	....	....	4 0	40 0	38 8	82 8
433	9	20	20	12	14	18	....	....	....	....	....	....	2 6	26 8	37 4	66 6
434	10-	16	24	17	11	16	10-	....	....	....	....	....	2 10	26 8	34 10	64 4
435	8-	10	17	21	15	12	....	....	....	....	....	....	2 3	26 8	29 7	58 6
436	8	12	19	20	17	....	....	....	....	....	....	....	2 8	40 0	35 0	77 8
437	8	18	12	19	10	....	....	....	....	....	....	....	2 6	26 8	31 4	60 6
438	9	16	21	11	23	10-	....	....	....	....	....	....	3 0	26 8	22 6	52 2
439	10-	20	19	12	16	16	12-	....	....	....	....	....	3 4	40 0	37 9	81 1
440	9	17	17	14	12	17	....	....	....	....	....	....	2 10	26 8	32 6	62 0
441	8-	19	12	21	17	12	....	....	....	....	....	....	3 0	40 0	25 7	68 7
442	8	13	16	19	19	8-	....	....	....	....	....	....	3 0	53 4	21 6	77 10
443	8-	17	22	20	11	16	....	....	....	....	....	....	2 3	26 8	26 3	55 2
444	11	11	24	19	20	17	10-	....	....	....	....	....	4 4	40 0	34 7	78 11
445	12	10	14	14	16	16	14	....	....	....	....	....	3 6	53 4	34 6	91 4
446	8	12	10	12	16		....	....	....	....	....	....	4 2	40 0	26 8	70 10
447	8-	14	20	17	11	10	....	....	....	....	....	....	3 6	40 0	21 4	64 10
448	8	13	19	17	12	7-	....	....	....	....	....	....	3 2	26 8	26 10	56 8
449	8	9	17	22	15	....	....	....	....	....	....	....	3 0	53 4	27 9	84 1
450	8	13	16	16	20	8-	....	....	....	....	....	....	4 0	40 0	23 9	67 9
451	9	16	20	23	19	12	....	....	....	....	....	....	4 8	66 8	26 4	97 8
452	8	10	14	19	19	....	....	....	....	....	....	....	2 2	26 8	24 6	53 4
453	9	12	16	21	17	11	....	....	....	....	....	....	3 0	26 8	27 4	57 0
454	8	11	13	26	12	5-	..	....	....	....	....	....	3 10	26 8	24 0	54 6
455	12	12	16	9	17	8	15	....	....	....	....	....	4 2	40 0	37 6	81 8
456	11	18	10	14	18	21	8-	....	....	....	....	....	3 4	40 0	40 4	83 8
457	8	18	18	19	12	7-	....	....	....	....	....	....	4 8	53 4	22 8	80 8
458	7	13	20	12	15	....	....	....	....	....	....	....	3 2	26 8	20 10	50 8
459	8	8	19	19	16	....	....	....	....	....	....	....	3 2	26 8	27 4	57 2
460	10	8	21	20	12	19	....	....	....	....	....	....	2 4	40 0	34 4	76 8
461	10	16	22	18	19	17	....	....	....	....	....	....	3 1	40 0	30 6	73 7
462	11-	14	19	21	21	11	14	....	....	....	....	....	4 0	40 0	31 10	75 10
463	10	11	20	17	19	19	....	....	....	....	....	....	3 4	40 0	29 8	73 0
464	8	10	17	19	23	...	....	....	....	....	....	....	2 8	40 0	21 9	64 5
465	9	16	12	14	20	10-	....	....	....	....	....	....	3 0	26 8	24 8	54 4
466	9	12	19	21	15	14	....	....	....	....	....	....	3 0	40 0	26 4	69 4
467	10	15	21	12	17	18	....	....	....	....	....	....	3 4	40 0	28 6	71 10
468	11	14	18	20	12	19	11	....	....	....	....	....	2 4	40 0	33 3	75 7
469	10	16	20	19	17	12	....	....	....	....	....	....	3 0	26 8	36 0	65 8
470	10	11	19	22	12	16	....	....	....	....	....	....	3 1	40 0	29 6	72 7
471	8	12	19	20	16	9-	....	....	....	....	....	....	3 8	53 4	23 5	80 5
472	8	11	16	19	22	....	....	....	....	....	....	....	3 0	40 0	24 8	67 8
473	7-	8	18	18	20	....	....	....	....	....	....	....	2 2	26 8	21 6	50 4
474	8	12	19	23	21	....	....	....	....	....	....	....	4 3	53 4	22 4	79 11
475	8	18	16	14	21	....	....	....	....	....	....	....	3 1	53 4	26 8	83 1
476	7	11	13	19	23	....	....	....	....	....	....	....	2 10	40 0	21 6	64 4
477	8	10	16	21	17	....	....	....	....	....	....	....	3 0	26 8	32 10	62 6
478	8-	12	19	19	10	13	....	....	....	....	....	....	3 6	40 0	21 8	65 2
479	9	14	14	20	11	13	....	....	....	....	....	....	3 0	26 8	33 0	62 8
480	9	13	19	9	16	2	....	....	....	....	....	....	3 1	40 0	34 6	77 7
481	9	12	21	17	16	20	....	....	....	....	....	....	4 4	40 0	30 8	75 0
482	8	10	17	12	20	....	....	....	....	....	....	....	2 2	26 8	20 10	49 8
483	8-	13	16	21	12	14	....	....	....	....	....	....	2 4	26 8	22 6	51 6
484	10	14	19	22	17	11	....	....	....	....	....	....	2 8	40 0	27 4	70 0
485	9	11	17	20	14	12	....	....	....	....	....	....	2 8	26 8	39 8	69 0
486	10	16	21	12	13	10	....	....	....	....	....	....	2 10	26 8	34 7	64 1
487	10	16	20	10	13	11	....	....	....	....	....	....	2 8	26 8	37 10	67 2
488	9	17	19	15	21	8	....	....	....	....	....	....	2 7	26 8	30 7	59 10
489	9	14	21	17	16	10	....	....	....	....	....	....	3 2	26 8	34 7	64 5
490	9	16	17	20	12	13	....	....	....	....	....	....	2 6	26 8	31 4	60 6
491	8	18	10	19	10	....	....	....	....	....	....	....	3 0	40 0	26 7	69 7
492	8	14	16	16	17	....	....	....	....	....	....	....	2 4	26 8	29 0	58 0
493	9	16	15	19	11	12	....	....	....	....	....	....	3 2	40 0	34 5	77 7
494	10	14	18	20	14	9	....	....	....	....	....	....	3 8	40 0	31 6	75 2
495	10	16	16	19	12	15	....	....	....	....	....	....	2 8	40 0	36 0	78 8
496	8	16	19	17	13	....	....	....	....	....	....	....	2 8	40 0	26 6	69 2
497	10	16	18	18	17	15	....	....	....	....	....	....	3 1	26 8	37 4	67 1

TABLE IV — (*Continued*).

SPECIMEN NUMBER.	Diameter of stump.	MEASUREMENTS ON STUMP. Number of rings per inch on stump, counting from the heart outward.																	Age in years.
498.....	1′ 1″	23	14	17	17	14	12	12											109
499.....	1 0	25	23	19	16	17	14	5-											119
500.....	1 2	31	27	22	19	18	17	15	15										164
501.....	1 0	25	26	22	12	16	12	7-											120
502.....	1 0	21	19	18	18	19	17												112
503.....	1 4	25	26	20	22	19	13	11	13	14									163
504.....	1 2	28	20	18	16	16	20	16	6-										140
505.....	1 4	24	28	12	12	13	16	15	11	8	7-								146
506.....	1 4	25	27	18	26	13	15	13	18	13									168
507.....	1 3	20	18	21	18	15	17	14	14										137
508.....	1 3	21	26	20	18	12	16	8	8	4-									135
509.....	1 0	20	24	18	26	25	30	7-											150
510.....	1 2	26	29	16	16	13	14	8	7										131
511.....	1 11	25	18	20	16	11	12	7	8	12	7	8	4-						149
512.....	1 1	25	36	21	18	20	17	20											157
513.....	1 4	21	24	18	20	15	16	13	12										140
514.....	1 3	22	16	14	13	14	15	14	15	11	11								145
515.....	1 0	30	12	28	20	21	12												133
516.....	1 0	22	40	30	23	24	12												151
517.....	1 4	15	20	31	18	13	11	18	16										142
518.....	1 0	24	20	19	20	21	18												122
519.....	1 0	32	24	31	21	19	15												145
520.....	1 0	29	21	19	19	17	22	11-											138
521.....	1 0	27	27	23	23	15	18												133
522.....	1 4	30	22	20	17	35	11	13	13										161
523.....	1 4	23	30	26	11	16	13	17	7	11									152
524.....	1 2	16	28	19	12	14	15	13	9	8	6								140
525.....	1 1	17	24	26	28	31	12	7-											145
526.....	1 1	31	23	25	13	10	17	11											130
527.....	1 1	31	29	19	16	13	17	12											137
528.....	1 4	11	14	22	25	18	19	23	17	7-									157
529.....	1 0	28	27	20	24	20	14	7-											140
530.....	1 1	20	16	19	27	24	12	18											136
531.....	1 2	27	19	16	15	23	21	19											140
532.....	1 0	33	26	19	11	17	18	12											136
533.....	1 1	31	26	24	18	25	19	12											158
534.....	1 1	23	21	14	18	15	16	12											122
535.....	1 1	36	33	18	18	11	16	12											144
536.....	1 0	27	21	26	13	18	17												122
537.....	1 0	26	22	20	14	16	12												110
538.....	1 4	28	16	12	16	20	13	15	10	9									139
539.....	1 2	21	20	14	16	11	14	15	27	9-									150
540.....	1 9	17	14	26	15	13	14	11	14	23	18								165
541.....	1 8	21	22	18	16	11	9	12	11	18	20	15							173
542.....	1 3	30	18	18	17	14	10	16	14										137
543.....	1 3	27	25	14	13	15	16	12	22	8-									152
544.....	1 1	23	19	12	20	23	21												127
545.....	1 3	27	19	16	23	24	17	19	21										166
546.....	1 2	30	25	19	12	8	9	19	8-										130
547.....	1 0	16	18	13	18	12	18												95
548.....	1 1	28	19	17	12	14	11	9-											105
549.....	1 2	33	27	19	12	17	13	10	11										142
550.....	1 0	27	16	19	18	12	11	8											106
551.....	1 1	24	23	29	16	17	18	12											139
552.....	1 3	36	33	20	14	17	26	17	11										174
553.....	1 0	24	12	26	12	7	18	17											116
554.....																			
555.....	1 4	20	30	13	11	14	15	11	21	10									145
556.....	1 1	20	21	17	15	17	21	23											134
557.....	1 0	21	12	13	16	18	18												98
558.....	1 5	12	14	18	11	14	15	18	14	18									174
559.....	1 2	11	16	19	17	18	20	30											131
560.....	1 1	28	19	15	17	12	17	14											142
561.....	1 10	16	6	5	8	11	13	11	12	12	10	14	16	20	14-				168
562.....	1 4	20	23	15	12	15	17	9	9	5-									125
563.....	1 0	14	21	18	14	19	25												111
564.....	1 0	21	18	17	17	21	13												107
565.....	1 2	16	18	11	15	12	11	16	15										114
566.....	1 2	25	19	12	14	9	16	14	7-										116
567.....	1 2	18	19	10	12	14	16	16	7-										112
568.....	1 4	16	21	12	10	13	12	14	14	12	6-								130

TABLE IV — (*Continued*).

SPECIMEN NUMBER *Continued.*	Diameter of top in inches.	Top Measurements. Number of rings per inch at top, counting from the heart outward.											Height of stump.	Combined length of logs.	Length of top.	Total height.
498	8	12	20	16	19								2' 8"	26' 8"	31' 7"	60' 11"
499	8	10	16	14	18								3 0	40 0	21 4	64 4
500	11	16	18	21	22	17	12						3 2	26 8	30 0	59 10
501	8	12	16	19	19								3 2	26 8	35 4	65 2
502	8-	16	14	20	16	9-							2 3	26 8	30 6	59 5
503	8-	17	19	12	18	10							3 0	53 4	22 7	78 11
504	10	12	20	17	19	11							3 2	40 0	31 10	75 0
505	10	16	19	19	12	17							3 3	40 0	36 8	79 11
506	10	14	14	12	23	20							3 1	40 0	32 6	75 7
507	10	16	19	18	10	16							2 10	26 8	41 3	70 9
508	10	17	17	19	22	18							3 1	40 0	40 2	83 3
509	8	13	19	12	21								2 6	40 0	36 6	79 0
510	8	16	7	21	20								3 2	40 0	27 4	70 6
511	12	7	7	11	9	16	13	18					3 0	40 0	40 6	83 6
512	11	18	20	16	18	18	14						2 10	13 4	43 7	59 9
513	10	16	20	8	12	17							2 8	40 0	34 4	77 0
514	8	12	16	19	16								3 2	53 4	24 6	81 0
515	8	13	18	17	21								2 6	26 8	21 5	50 7
516	8	10	12	20	12								3 1	40 0	26 10	69 11
517	9	10	12	14	18	22							3 4	40 0	31 7	74 11
518	8	10	14	18	18								2 6	40 0	22 6	65 0
519	8	11	16	16	23								2 8	40 0	23 4	66 0
520	8	10	17	17	21								3 0	40 0	23 7	66 7
521	8	13	16	20	20								3 0	40 0	21 6	64 6
522	7	10	10	13	17								3 3	53 4	22 4	78 11
523	8	11	16	19	15								4 0	53 4	30 0	87 4
524	8	12	14	20	20								2 10	40 0	28 6	71 4
525	10	16	11	15	13	10							3 2	26 8	41 7	71 5
526	10	14	18	20	12	17							2 8	26 8	43 4	72 8
527	11	16	16	19	22	15							3 0	40 0	26 8	69 8
528	9	17	17	21	20	12							2 8	26 8	31 0	60 4
529	8	18	21	17	13	6-							2 10	26 6	37 3	66 7
530	9	13	19	16	15	11							2 11	40 0	28 4	71 3
531	10	19	24	18	12	16							3 4	40 0	30 6	73 10
532	9	18	12	23	19	17							3 0	26 8	29 6	59 2
533	9	16	16	19	17	20							3 3	26 8	34 0	63 11
534	9	16	18	22	21	10-							4 0	40 0	31 6	75 6
535	8	14	19	11	23								3 0	26 8	28 4	58 0
536	9	18	18	16	16	15							2 10	26 8	39 0	68 6
537	10	16	19	16	18	21							3 0	40 0	26 10	69 10
538	10	17	18	20	17	18							3 1	26 8	31 6	61 3
539	8	18	23	21	16								4 2	53 4	19 10	77 4
540	9	18	19	22	17	17							4 0	53 4	22 6	79 10
541	8-	16	20	21	19	12							3 4	40 0	36 4	79 8
542	9	17	22	16	23	13-							3 0	40 0	34 8	77 8
543	9	12	17	17	21	11							3 2	26 8	27 4	57 2
544	9	16	19	12	17	11							3 7	26 8	31 5	61 8
545	8	19	14	17	12	6-							3 4	26 8	33 2	63 2
546	7	21	17	16	8-								3 9	40 0	26 4	70 1
547	11	23	21	16	12	9	6-						3 6	40 0	31 6	75 0
548	10	24	17	11	10	16							3 1	53 4	27 4	83 9
549	10	12	19	17	8	13	5-						3 8	40 0	31 7	75 3
550	9	14	13	11	19	21							3 6	40 0	27 4	70 10
551	8	16	17	10	14	7-							3 3	40 0	31 4	74 7
552	8	18	19	21	17								3 1	26 8	30 4	60 1
553	8-	12	16	19	20	8-							2 10	26 8	31 10	61 4
554																
555	10-	17	19	23	19	10	11						2 10	40 0	33 0	75 10
556	7	16	14	19	22								3 0	40 0	28 4	71 4
557	8	18	15	17	19								2 10	26 8	26 0	55 6
558	10-	10	12	17	22	20	19						3 0	26 8	39 8	69 4
559	8	8	10	13	19	12-							2 10	40 0	24 10	67 8
560	8	9	11	19	17								2 6	40 0	31 4	73 10
561	11	7	10	16	19	22	17-						3 7	53 4	34 8	91 7
562	11	10	11	12	21	21	8-						3 4	26 8	48 6	78 6
563	8-	8	13	12	19	13							3 1	26 8	43 8	73 5
564	8-	12	12	9	17	8-							2 8	26 8	28 4	57 8
565	10	10	14	21	20	13							3 4	26 8	37 10	67 10
566	10	12	12	7	23	16							2 6	26 8	34 5	63 7
567	11	18	12	21	22	16	16						3 2	26 8	37 6	67 4
568	12	0	10	17	19	24	17						3 0	26 8	41 4	71 0

Table IV — (*Continued*).

Specimen Number.	Diameter of stump.	Measurements on Stump. Number of rings per inch on stump, counting from the heart outward.																	Age in years.
569.....	1′ 5″	12	6	9	12	24	18	10	14	15	11	....	....	....	....	....	....	....	131
570.....	1 5	13	11	24	14	8	9	16	19	13	....	....	....	....	....	....	....	....	127
571.....	1 2	14	11	15	13	13	18	14	12	....	....	....	....	....	....	....	....	....	120
572.....	1 6	12	6	7	7	10	13	18	17	20	22	....	....	....	....	....	....	....	132
573.....	1 8	9	6	5	5	5	7	12	16	20	24	14-	....	....	....	....	....	....	138
574.....	1 3	20	10	15	16	16	14	12	12	11	5-	....	....	....	....	....	....	....	137
575.....	1 4	17	17	14	22	22	13	8	8	6	....	....	....	....	....	....	....	....	129
576.....	1 2	14	19	25	17	15	20	17	22	....	....	....	....	....	....	....	....	....	149
577.....	1 1	20	24	26	13	12	12	9	4-	....	....	....	....	....	....	....	....	....	1[illegible]0
578.....	1 2	20	24	22	14	9	11	9	9	4-	....	....	....	....	....	....	....	....	[illegible]
579.....	1 2	14	22	23	16	19	15	10	19	....	....	....	....	....	....	....	....	....	148
580.....	1 3	16	22	18	15	21	16	10	17	13	....	....	....	....	....	....	....	....	151
581.....	1 0	21	21	19	18	20	20	22	....	....	....	....	....	....	....	....	....	....	141
582.....	1 4	13	16	18	16	9	14	15	18	28	....	....	....	....	....	....	....	....	147
583.....	1 3	17	23	24	17	19	19	23	21	....	....	....	....	....	....	....	....	....	160
584.....	1 0	20	26	21	23	15	16	9	....	....	....	....	....	....	....	....	....	....	130
585.....	1 2	12	15	22	16	18	20	19	18	....	....	....	....	....	....	....	....	....	140
586.....	1 4	11	8	11	14	19	18	20	21	12-	....	....	....	....	....	....	....	....	137
587.....	1 0	25	18	13	16	15	18	....	....	....	....	....	....	....	....	....	....	....	105
588.....	1 2	15	40	24	12	14	17	19	20	....	....	....	....	....	....	....	....	....	161
589.....	1 1	14	26	27	21	12	21	10	....	....	....	....	....	....	....	....	....	....	112
590.....	1 1	12	18	26	21	25	22	18	12	....	....	....	....	....	....	....	....	....	137
591.....	1 2	14	9	8	14	24	28	30	....	....	....	....	....	....	....	....	....	....	127
592.....	1 3	12	15	24	23	27	19	21	30	....	....	....	....	....	....	....	....	....	171
593.....	1 6	12	12	8	18	19	19	18	15	20	28	....	....	....	....	....	....	....	174
594.....	1 2	16	26	25	21	13	22	28	14	....	....	....	....	....	....	....	....	....	167
595.....	1 0	16	17	28	26	22	24	....	....	....	....	....	....	....	....	....	....	....	143
596.....	1 2	15	18	20	15	20	21	18	13	....	....	....	....	....	....	....	....	....	140
597.....	1 4	12	24	15	14	12	13	16	14	4-	....	....	....	....	....	....	....	....	134
598.....	1 0	18	27	28	24	18	6	6	....	....	....	....	....	....	....	....	....	....	127
599.....	1 4	15	12	9	10	12	16	24	21	18	....	....	....	....	....	....	....	....	137
600.....	1 8	10	16	12	13	12	11	10	11	13	16	10	....	....	....	....	....	....	144
601.....	1 1	14	24	21	18	18	14	12	11	....	....	....	....	....	....	....	....	....	132
602.....	1 0	18	16	20	16	13	12	12	....	....	....	....	....	....	....	....	....	....	117
603.....	1 0	18	17	18	20	14	15	9	9	....	....	....	....	....	....	....	....	....	120
604.....	1 0	14	14	16	24	16	11	14	....	....	....	....	....	....	....	....	....	....	109
605.....	1 0	18	16	13	15	18	24	28	....	....	....	....	....	....	....	....	....	....	132
606.....	1 2	21	14	16	15	17	14	12	14	....	....	....	....	....	....	....	....	....	191
607.....	1 3	13	14	28	21	16	14	12	14	14	....	....	....	....	....	....	....	....	146
608.....	1 0	18	14	23	22	21	24	26	....	....	....	....	....	....	....	....	....	....	152
609.....	1 2	19	13	18	17	11	9	18	12	....	....	....	....	....	....	....	....	....	117
610.....	1 5	14	11	13	15	12	17	18	19	33	....	....	....	....	....	....	....	....	152
611.....	1 4	10	14	15	17	14	14	21	16	18	12	6-	....	....	....	....	....	....	163
612.....	1 2	15	16	24	17	20	18	23	6-	....	....	....	....	....	....	....	....	....	141
613.....	1 0	13	9	14	24	21	26	....	....	....	....	....	....	....	....	....	....	....	106
614.....	1 4	15	18	19	20	14	22	20	16	....	....	....	....	....	....	....	....	....	144
615.....	1 1	17	16	17	20	22	12	18	21	....	....	....	....	....	....	....	....	....	141
616.....	1 8	2	28	16	19	14	13	17	15	18	6	15	19	18	....	....	....	....	230
617.....	1 4	17	13	19	17	14	22	17	18	....	....	....	....	....	....	....	....	....	137
618.....	1 5	10	14	12	15	12	14	8	16	20	....	....	....	....	....	....	....	....	121
619.....	1 6	9	6	9	12	19	19	10	15	18	12	12	....	....	....	....	....	....	141
620.....	1 3	10	11	14	13	20	19	16	18	16	....	....	....	....	....	....	....	....	131
621.....	1 1	2	12	17	19	19	15	12	....	....	....	....	....	....	....	....	....	....	.05
622.....	1 0	18	15	26	22	19	9	16	....	....	....	....	....	....	....	....	....	....	125
623.....	1 0	15	17	20	23	15	15	....	....	....	....	....	....	....	....	....	....	....	105
624.....	1 0	19	23	21	30	24	19	....	....	....	....	....	....	....	....	....	....	....	133
625.....	1 0	22	29	26	24	19	12	....	....	....	....	....	....	....	....	....	....	....	132
626.....	1 0	23	21	18	21	22	17	....	....	....	....	....	....	....	....	....	....	....	122
627.....	1 2	20	16	20	15	30	14	16	13	5-	....	....	....	....	....	....	....	....	149
628.....	1 1	18	17	14	21	17	15	12	....	....	....	....	....	....	....	....	....	....	115
629 ...	1 0	24	20	10	17	8	9	8	....	....	....	....	....	....	....	....	....	....	105
630.....	1 0	13	21	18	16	15	17	....	....	....	....	....	....	....	....	....	....	....	110
631.....	1 1	13	13	16	17	12	17	23	7-	....	....	....	....	....	....	....	....	....	118
632.....	1 5	15	19	23	18	18	13	15	12	18	....	....	....	....	....	....	....	....	151
633.....	1 1	16	15	16	17	13	14	14	20	7-	....	....	....	....	....	....	....	....	131
634.....	1 3	20	30	24	19	13	15	13	13	....	....	....	....	....	....	....	....	....	147
635.....	1 1	35	22	21	28	23	16	12	....	....	....	....	....	....	....	....	....	....	177
636.....	1 6	16	16	19	18	19	15	13	15	23	....	....	....	....	....	....	....	....	153
637.....	1 1	19	14	19	24	16	27	36	....	....	....	....	....	....	....	....	....	....	155
638.....	1 3	21	17	29	24	12	13	16	13	16	....	....	....	....	....	....	....	....	160
639.....	1 8	32	19	16	13	18	21	18	20	18	25	28	....	....	....	....	....	....	238

Table IV — (*Continued*).

SPECIMEN NUMBER *Continued.*	Diameter of top in inches.	Top Measurements. Number of rings per inch at top, counting from the heart outward.											Height of stump.	Combined length of logs.	Length of top.	Total height.
569.....	11	7	12	16	16	21	18	....	....	....	....	....	3′ 5″	40′ 0″	36′ 10″	80′ 3″
570.....	10	10	12	12	21	22	....	....	....	....	....	....	3 4	40 0	28 6	71 10
571.....	10	11	14	22	17	19	....	....	....	....	....	....	4 1	26 8	43 0	73 9
572.....	9	12	17	19	21	23	....	....	....	....	....	....	4 1	40 0	36 2	80 3
573.....	9	12	14	17	19	19	....	....	....	....	....	....	4 2	53 4	27 8	85 2
574.....	8	8	13	16	22	....	....	....	....	....	....	....	2 10	40 0	21 6	64 4
575.....	9	16	10	21	14	11	....	....	....	....	....	....	2 6	26 8	33 6	61 8
576.....	8	11	12	17	21	....	....	....	....	....	....	....	2 3	40 0	21 0	63 3
577.....	8	12	10	19	10	....	....	....	....	....	....	....	2 6	26 8	25 4	54 6
578.....	8	16	11	9	9	....	....	....	....	....	....	....	3 10	40 0	24 6	68 4
579.....	8	12	16	20	13	....	....	....	....	....	....	....	3 8	40 0	27 0	70 8
580.....	8	13	15	19	16	....	....	....	....	....	....	....	2 7	40 0	23 4	65 11
581.....	7-	14	12	17	17	....	....	....	....	....	....	....	2 1	40 0	16 3	58 4
582.....	8	8	11	14	19	....	....	....	....	....	....	....	2 8	53 4	22 6	78 6
583.....	8-	10	12	16	10	8	....	....	....	....	....	....	2 6	40 0	28 7	71 1
584.....	8	14	12	17	11	....	....	....	....	....	....	....	2 9	26 8	24 10	54 3
585.....	10	16	16	19	12	9	....	....	....	....	....	....	3 3	26 8	26 3	56 2
586.....	8	10	12	17	12	....	....	....	....	....	....	....	4 0	53 4	20 7	77 11
587.....	7	14	11	13	9	....	....	....	....	....	....	....	3 1	26 8	22 4	52 1
588.....	9	16	20	14	14	12	....	....	....	....	....	....	2 2	26 8	20 7	49 5
589.....	8	17	19	17	16	....	....	....	....	....	....	....	3 4	40 0	21 4	64 8
590.....	7	16	12	18	13	....	....	....	....	....	....	....	2 8	40 0	23 4	66 0
591.....	8	12	9	21	17	....	....	....	....	....	....	....	2 3	40 0	27 6	69 9
592.....	8	12	17	16	16	....	....	....	....	....	....	....	2 10	40 0	28 4	71 2
593.....	8	8	11	19	12	....	....	....	....	....	....	....	2 6	53 4	18 8	74 6
594.....	8	12	13	21	11	....	....	....	....	....	....	....	3 0	53 4	21 4	77 8
595.....	8	12	14	14	19	....	....	....	....	....	....	....	2 8	26 8	24 7	53 11
596.....	8-	14	14	21	20	....	....	....	....	....	....	....	3 2	40 0	21 6	64 8
597.....	8	14	19	17	14	....	....	....	....	....	....	....	2 8	40 0	19 8	62 4
598.....	8	12	9	21	12	....	....	....	....	....	....	....	2 8	26 8	23 3	52 7
599.....	9	11	13	19	16	10	....	....	....	....	....	....	3 1	53 4	27 10	84 3
600.....	8	10	4	22	17	6-	....	....	....	....	....	....	4 0	53 4	23 9	81 1
601.....	11	17	16	21	18	18	12	....	....	....	....	....	3 6	13 4	48 2	65 0
602.....	8	8	11	17	12	....	....	....	....	....	....	....	3 2	40 0	21 6	64 8
603.....	8	10	10	14	14	....	....	....	....	....	....	....	2 6	26 8	27 0	56 2
604.....	8	12	12	12	9	....	....	....	....	....	....	....	3 0	40 0	28 6	71 6
605.....	8	16	13	10	8	....	....	....	....	....	....	....	3 1	26 8	30 4	60 1
606.....	8-	10	10	16	13	9	....	....	....	....	....	....	2 11	40 0	29 6	72 5
607.....	9	10	13	14	13	13	....	....	....	....	....	....	3 3	40 0	30 4	73 7
608.....	9	11	13	16	13	15	....	....	....	....	....	....	2 4	26 8	27 6	56 6
609.....	8	11	12	14	16	....	....	....	....	....	....	....	3 6	40 0	21 4	64 10
610.....	9	12	12	17	17	19	....	....	....	....	....	....	3 2	40 0	26 6	69 8
611.....	10	12	14	16	16	10	....	....	....	....	....	....	2 10	26 8	30 4	59 10
612.....	8	12	9	14	17	....	....	....	....	....	....	....	3 1	40 0	23 6	66 7
613.....	8	8	11	16	12	....	....	....	....	....	....	....	2 11	16 8	21 9	51 4
614.....	8	9	9	23	11	....	....	....	....	....	....	....	2 7	40 0	19 8	62 3
615.....	8	8	14	16	16	....	....	....	....	....	....	....	3 4	40 0	25 10	69 2
616.....	9	12	14	16	21	13	....	....	....	....	....	....	2 8	53 4	22 3	78 3
617.....	11	15	15	11	14	16	14	9-	....	....	....	....	3 0	26 8	38 10	68 6
618.....	10	16	17	14	14	12	....	....	....	....	....	....	3 2	40 0	34 11	78 1
619.....	10	16	18	11	10	14	....	....	....	....	....	....	2 8	40 0	28 8	71 4
620.....	8	14	14	16	15	....	....	....	....	....	....	....	2 10	53 4	25 10	82 0
621.....	8	9	11	17	16	....	....	....	....	....	....	....	2 9	26 8	30 0	59 5
622.....	8	10	13	16	13	....	....	....	....	....	....	....	3 0	26 8	32 3	61 11
623.....	8	10	11	10	16	....	....	....	....	....	....	....	2 10	26 8	31 7	61 1
624.....	8	11	11	17	17	....	....	....	....	....	....	....	2 10	26 8	30 0	59 6
625.....	8	10	17	19	16	....	....	....	....	....	....	....	2 9	26 8	30 4	59 9
626.....	10	11	10	16	15	17	....	....	....	....	....	....	3 2	26 8	27 8	57 6
627.....	8-	11	12	12	14	8	....	....	....	....	....	....	3 0	40 0	32 0	75 0
628.....	8	13	11	16	15	....	....	....	....	....	....	....	2 8	40 0	32 6	75 2
629.....	8	14	12	12	14	....	....	....	....	....	....	....	3 0	26 8	34 8	64 4
630.....	8	9	11	17	12	....	....	....	....	....	....	....	2 4	26 8	23 6	52 6
631.....	10	8	10	11	15	16	....	....	....	....	....	....	3 10	26 8	36 4	66 10
632.....	8½	11	14	13	11	17	....	....	....	....	....	....	3 2	40 0	31 3	74 5
633.....	8	11	11	15	15	7-	....	....	....	....	....	....	2 10	40 0	27 6	70 4
634.....	10	10	12	16	19	10	....	....	....	....	....	....	2 8	40 0	34 4	77 0
635.....	8	10	12	14	17	....	....	....	....	....	....	....	2 10	40 0	26 10	69 8
636.....	8	10	10	16	16	....	....	....	....	....	....	....	3 0	53 4	21 6	77 10
637.....	8	13	16	19	12	....	....	....	....	....	....	....	2 8	40 0	24 10	67 6
638.....	10	12	17	17	14	12	....	....	....	....	....	....	2 8	40 0	36 7	79 3
639.....	10	16	19	12	16	8	7-	....	....	....	....	....	4 0	53 4	33 0	90 4

TABLE IV — (*Continued*).

SPECIMEN NUMBER.	Diameter of stump.	MEASUREMENTS ON STUMP. Number of rings per inch on stump, counting from the heart outward.																	Age in years.
640	1′ 2″	14	20	23	22	18	20	28											145
641	1 2	16	12	14	24	20	20	16	14										126
642	1 4	15	16	15	18	13	16	16	14	8-									131
643	2 0	8	7	7	8	8	12	13	13	17	14	19	22	32					180
644	1 6	14	8	9	14	12	12	11	17	20	19	10							145
645	1 6	13	9	8	15	16	15	13	16	24	28								157
646	1 4	12	9	10	15	14	15	19	23	31	15-								166
647	1 4	14	9	10	16	20	18	19	22	30									158
648	1 6	16	11	10	19	15	16	16	19	25	16-								163
649	1 4	15	12	12	14	16	21	22	30										142
650	1 6	12	13	19	14	10	14	12	20	21									135
651	1 0	16	17	18	16	16	15												98
652	1 2	14	22	20	15	12	12	18	9-										122
653	1 3	10	13	25	9	8	16	15	25	25									146
654	1 4	10	5	7	11	17	12	16	14	31	11-								134
655	1 0	20	21	21	18	17	19												119
656	1 0	27	15	20	19	18	19	17-											135
657	1 0	25	20	21	18	16	13	7-											120
658	1 4	18	17	17	17	14	14	10	15	35									157
659	1 3	12	20	10	14	11	14	20	16										117
660	1 5	12	18	19	14	16	15	13	13	11									131
661	1 4	18	24	23	17	16	13	16	11										138
662	1 8	26	30	20	15	14	14	10	9	8	10								150
663	1 0	24	21	22	18	24	28												137
664	1 1	26	21	23	18	18	19	15	7-										150
665	1 2	34	26	22	17	24	20	26	24										193
666	1 1	33	28	12	12	23	23	25	24										188
667	1 1	25	21	15	18	22	24	2-											153
668	1 1	14	28	24	27	26	22	14											1[illegible]5
669	1 0	24	24	19	21	26	24	14-											166
670	1 2	18	29	30	2[illegible]	23	23	16											160
671	1 6	20	19	10	11	10	13	10	11	14	14	23							155
672	1 0	23	27	27	24	23	16	14											153
673	1 0	21	21	20	15	13	15												108
674	1 0	20	18	22	30	13	19	10											132
675	1 5	22	34	16	12	12	9	12	15	14-									146
676	1 2	23	17	22	10	14	10	21	16-										147
677	1 6	23	25	28	16	14	16	18	10	7									157
678	1 2	21	25	18	14	16	9	6	11										120
679	1 1	33	17	19	15	16	10	5-											118
680	1 4	26	27	24	23	18	16	20	14										168
681	1 6	25	26	30	12	16	14	18	8	12	20								174
682	1 2	34	27	42	30	17	18	14	28	10-									214
683	1 3	33	30	24	15	15	12	17	13	8									167
684	1 1	40	35	25	18	12	14	14	9-										167
685	1 3	26	18	15	9	10	9	13	20	10									139
686	1 5	22	29	15	10	12	6	8	10	16	12-								140
687	2 0	24	20	22	15	11	8	9	14	11	15	14	12	20					195
688	1 2	32	22	18	21	19	22	19	8-										161
689	1 1	28	18	23	16	23	19	16											137
690	1 6	21	22	8	8	13	10	19	17	21	11								163
691	1 1	26	13	15	21	17	16	17											125
692	1 3	11	8	10	11	17	17	21	20										115
693	1 8	22	21	21	16	15	19	11	9	8	8								158
694	1 8	37	44	29	17	15	26	24	15										217
695	1 8	24	18	28	17	16	10	1[illegible]	19	17	20	30							210
696	1 1	18	16	15	16	11	13	10	6										105
697	1 1	28	24	26	21	18	18	9-											142
698	1 0	28	26	21	21	19	14												129
699	1 2	22	20	18	21	18	15	7	1[illegible]										128
700	1 4	23	26	18	19	18	11	9	8	8	8								148
701	1 3	40	20	11	16	17	11	9	19	5-									148
702	1 1	25	22	17	16	18	24	23											145
703	1 8	16	20	24	12	9	16	12	15	16	19	5-							164
704	1 6	28	25	13	14	10	14	19	16	12	9	9							109
705	1 0	17	14	18	19	18	15												101
706	1 9	24	23	20	16	18	15	16	14	16	17	10							189
707	1 2	20	22	28	26	32	29	19	11										187
708	1 1	30	23	19	16	13	9	10	5-										125
709	1 2	32	21	26	16	17	11	12											135
710	1 4	22	18	16	20	14	14	10	16	7									137

TABLE IV — (*Continued*).

SPECIMEN NUMBER *Continued.*	Diameter of top in inches.	Top Measurements. Number of rings per inch at top, counting from the heart outward.											Height of stump.	Combined length of logs.	Length of top.	Total height.
640	10	15	12	14	19	9							3′ 4″	40′ 0″	34′ 8″	78′ 0″
641	9	14	14	16	18	12							2 10	40 0	39 0	81 10
642	11	14	15	9	11	17	9-						3 6	40 0	42 6	86 0
643	11	15	15	16	12	16	12						3 0	53 4	36 9	93 1
644	8	10	13	15	19								3 3	53 4	32 4	88 11
645	8	12	16	17	19								3 2	53 4	26 7	83 1
646	9	16	12	12	14	7-							3 4	53 4	24 6	81 2
647	8	11	12	16	14								3 0	53 4	26 3	82 7
648	10	11	12	12	15	15							2 8	53 4	28 6	84 6
649	9	11	12	16	14	9-							4 4	53 4	26 0	83 8
650	6	13	13	12	17								3 10	53 4	19 8	76 10
651	8	8	10	14	13								3 0	40 0	21 2	64 2
652	8	8	11	16	12								3 2	40 0	28 7	71 9
653	7	8	12	14	12								4 1	53 4	21 0	78 5
654	8	8	11	20	16								2 4	53 4	23 6	79 2
655	8	8	12	14	17								4 0	26 8	24 8	55 4
656	8	11	13	16	16								3 0	26 8	27 0	56 8
657	8	10	14	12	13	6-							3 8	40 0	21 6	65 2
658	12½	16	17	16	18	11	14	11-					3 8	26 8	38 0	68 4
659	9	11	12	17	17	10							3 10	40 0	32 7	76 5
660	8	11	11	16	14								4 0	40 0	31 6	75 6
661	9	11	16	20	15	8-							3 0	40 0	30 0	73 0
662	8	12	14	17	11								3 10	53 4	18 4	75 6
663	8	11	16	16	13								4 0	26 8	23 6	54 2
664	8	12	14	15	11								3 4	40 0	26 8	70 0
665	7-	10	15	12	13								4 1	53 4	30 7	88 0
666	8	10	16	14	12								2 10	40 0	26 0	68 10
667	8	12	14	14	15								3 0	40 0	22 6	65 6
668	8	11	16	13	17								2 10	40 0	28 4	71 2
669	10	12	13	13	16	16							2 10	26 8	34 6	64 0
670	7	10	14	14	16								4 2	53 4	18 8	76 2
671	8	11	12	15	15								2 8	53 4	21 7	77 7
672	8	14	9	12	16								2 10	40 0	27 3	70 1
673	9	10	16	15	8	12							2 10	40 0	27 11	70 9
674	9	11	14	17	11	8-							3 2	26 8	38 6	68 4
675	10	16	11	13	12	16							2 6	40 0	31 6	74 0
676	10	16	10	16	13	11							2 6	26 8	39 0	68 2
677	10	15	13	13	13	10							2 8	40 0	27 0	69 8
678	8	12	12	16	10								2 2	40 0	27 6	69 8
679	9	12	10	14	8	8-							2 10	26 8	27 10	57 4
680	11	12	16	16	9	8	7-						3 0	26 8	28 4	53 0
681	8	14	11	17	10								3 2	53 4	15 8	72 2
682	9-	15	16	12	11	11							3 4	40 0	27 8	71 0
683	9	13	14	14	8	7-							2 10	40 0	32 4	75 2
684	10	14	14	12	18	12							2 10	26 8	27 6	57 0
685	8	11	17	10	11	6-							2 4	40 0	21 7	63 11
686	11	10	11	12	13	15	17						3 2	26 8	26 6	56 4
687	9	10	12	13	12	16							4 4	53 4	23 8	81 4
688	9	12	13	14	16	10							3 8	40 0	30 0	73 8
689	8	9	13	16	16								2 6	40 0	26 8	69 2
690	11	12	12	16	15	8	8-						2 10	40 0	28 6	71 4
691	8	13	12	10	15								2 10	40 0	31 4	74 2
692	7	10	14	12	10-								2 10	53 4	19 4	75 6
693	8	10	13	10	10								2 6	40 0	23 0	65 6
694	8-	13	17	18	9	11							2 4	40 0	21 6	63 10
695	11	11	14	10	22	16	19						4 0	53 4	30 3	87 7
696	8	12	12	10	10								2 10	26 8	25 4	54 10
697	9	11	16	9	9	9-							3 0	40 0	32 10	75 10
698	8	8	18	12	12								2 8	26 8	36 6	65 10
699	8	10	14	15	10								2 4	40 0	25 4	67 8
700	8	16	2	14	8								3 2	40 0	28 3	71 5
701	8	12	9	13	13								2 8	40 0	18 6	61 2
702	8	13	16	15	12								2 8	26 8	26 4	55 8
703	9-	14	16	16	22	24							2 4	40 0	24 0	66 4
704	9	16	16	15	23	23							2 0	40 0	30 4	72 4
705	8	13	17	14	20								1 10	26 8	36 0	64 6
706	12	15	16	17	22	21	12						3 0	40 0	34 4	77 4
707	9	16	16	19	18	17							2 4	40 0	28 10	71 2
708	7-	14	18	18	19								1 10	26 8	33 6	62 0
709	8	12	13	16	16								2 2	40 0	23 4	64 6
710	8	13	13	18	17								2 4	53 4	23 6	79 2

TABLE IV — (*Continued*).

Specimen number.	Diameter of stump.	Measurements on Stump.																	Age in years.
		Number of rings per inch on stump, counting from the heart outward.																	
711	1′ 1″	21	20	25	15	11	9	14											115
712	1 1	22	18	11	10	11	17	27											111
713	1 2	24	16	14	18	16	14	8											110
714	1 0	23	25	34	20	29	18												142
715	1 0	23	21	24	24	12	10												117
716	1 3	22	40	30	21	20	20	11	15										179
717	1 8	34	23	17	22	12	18	21	12	15	14	20	24						235
718	1 7	30	18	15	22	18	20	17	17	11	5–								173
719	1 8	25	16	15	17	15	11	15	13	14	18	20	18						197
720	1 8	23	16	18	13	16	14	9	7	11	8	10							152
721	1 7	26	30	27	14	13	10	8	12	7	9	8							164
722	1 6	21	20	21	21	24	31	9	10	20	14								194
723	1 0	30	23	21	24	20	24												147
724	1 0	31	30	20	24	21	25												151
725	1 0	26	27	12	14	23	10												181
726	1 0	20	22	19	16	11	9												97
727	1 2	23	30	24	17	16	10	12	5–										137
728	1 0	30	15	17	15	17	14												108
729	1 0	33	16	15	19	17	14												114
730	1 1	35	20	21	27	13	15	13	6–										159
731	1 1	36	33	26	27	20	11	15											167
732	1 4	22	15	16	16	14	16	15	20	27									161
733	1 1	34	30	22	23	23	20	18	8										178
734	1 5	24	22	15	15	17	15	18	16	17									159
735	1 1	29	17	18	17	12	9	9											111
736	1 0	30	21	21	15	15	16	5–											123
737	1 1	34	15	13	13	15	17	15											121
738	1 0	21	18	28	26	28	26												147
739	1 1	28	26	18	13	12	8–												115
740	1 8	25	34	19	18	11	17	11	15	20	17								187
741	1 0	25	13	18	15	19	15												105
742	1 4	20	16	17	21	14	14	12	12										128
743	1 8	22	28	19	38	21	14	12	15	17	14	10–							210
744	1 5	34	40	20	27	10	10	13	18	20									185
745	1 0	32	24	28	26	14	9	5–											138
746	1 1	36	21	24	19	12	11	11	13										147
747	1 5	16	16	20	22	19	12	11	10	9									135
748	1 1	33	14	16	22	16	16	15	8–										140
749	1 12	20	30	25	13	8	14	12	10										132
750	1 3	24	23	17	15	14	16	11	8–										128
751	1 1	40	19	20	26	17	9	11	21										163
752	1 10	19	16	21	9	15	15	15	15	12	22–								159
753	1 2	27	22	27	17	16	15	19											145
754	1 1	18	21	20	15	15	11	19	8–										127
755	1 0	21	30	26	27	15	23												141
756	1 8	27	14	12	12	11	12	14	19	17	18	25							181
757	1 10	32	16	20	23	21	13	9	11	7	15	13							120
758	1 8	35	26	31	15	10	10	13	11	11	16	12–							190
759	1 3	32	25	18	15	16	17	16	13										152
760	1 4	25	24	15	14	12	12	13	8	10									133
761	1 3	36	28	21	11	15	20	19	13										163
762	1 3	30	33	28	9	11	13	12	19	10–									165
763	1 2	28	33	17	11	13	11	18	13										144
764	1 7	36	29	24	17	14	15	11	9	8	6–								169
765	1 3	17	15	29	30	33	30	19	16										189
766	1 6	22	26	12	10	10	14	14	16	12									136
767	1 6	17	27	20	16	12	16	16	18	11	11								164
768	1 1	24	27	22	14	13	14	28											142
769	1 6	17	14	19	10	11	11	10	14	19	20								145
770	1 8	22	20	21	13	9	11	13	13	13	15	17							167
771	1 0	42	34	22	14	11	10												133
772	1 1	32	23	22	10	14	8	8	10										127
773	1 3	26	22	25	30	25	22	27	28										205
774	1 1	21	17	26	37	18	15	13											148
775	1 7	23	26	19	12	13	20	16	14	11	10								161
776	1 1	32	33	30	24	8	9	6–											142
777	1 4	31	16	19	18	20	25	30	31										193
778	1 0	30	20	24	23	16	14												126
779	1 2	26	15	14	15	15	16	11	12										124
780	1 2	20	19	15	16	15	13	15	16										129
781	1 1	28	19	24	19	14	11	9	7										130
782	1 0	14	18	17	13	30	14												106

TABLE IV — (*Continued*).

SPECIMEN NUMBER *Continued.*	Diameter of top in inches.	Top Measurements. Number of rings per inch at top, counting from the heart outward.											Height of stump.	Combined length of logs.	Length of top.	Total height.
711	8–	16	13	15	16	7–							2′ 2″	26′ 8″	38′ 4″	67′ 2″
712	8	11	14	15	16								2 1	31 8	22 6	56 3
713	9	10	8	15	13	12							1 8	26 8	42 6	70 10
714	9	13	6	22	20	16							1 10	13 4	45 10	61 0
715	9	15	16	19	21	10–							1 6	13 4	46 4	61 2
716	9	14	18	18	17	12							2 2	40 0	32 7	74 9
717	11	8	14	23	21	20	19						2 6	53 4	27 0	82 10
718	9	8	9	17	24	23	11–						2 6	53 4	26 0	81 10
719	10	10	9	16	20	24							3 0	66 8	21 4	91 0
720	9	11	12	14	17	17							3 0	66 8	23 6	93 2
721	8–	12	12	12	16	19							2 4	66 8	22 8	91 8
722	10	13	12	16	18	9							2 8	53 4	24 0	80 0
723	8	13	12	12	16								2 0	26 8	30 0	58 8
724	8	14	10	13	13								1 6	26 8	30 8	58 10
725	8	14	16	13	12								2 0	26 8	33 9	62 5
726	8	11	14	14	14								1 10	26 8	31 4	59 10
727	10	11	11	16	17	14							2 0	26 8	39 10	68 6
728	8½	11	10	15	18	7–							2 8	26 8	40 0	69 4
729	8	13	11	12	16								2 6	26 8	37 8	66 10
730	8	11	14	14	15								2 4	40 0	27 6	69 10
731	7–	10	10	16	12								1 8	26 8	29 4	57 8
732	9–	13	12	14	16	9–							2 8	40 0	34 10	77 6
733	7	12	16	14	14								2 4	40 0	32 6	74 10
734	8	16	17	16	12								2 6	53 4	24 0	79 10
735	9	11	13	17	11	9–							2 6	26 8	36 10	66 0
736	8	12	12	14	15								1 10	13 4	48 6	63 8
737	8	12	14	15	16								2 3	26 8	34 9	63 8
738	8	14	13	10	19								3 2	26 8	28 4	58 2
739	8½	13	17	16	12	8–							2 0	26 8	29 0	57 8
740	8	14	16	16	12								2 4	53 4	26 6	82 2
741	8	10	11	17	13								2 0	26 8	28 0	56 8
742	10	11	13	16	13	12							2 1	40 0	31 10	73 11
743	10	13	16	14	16	13							3 3	53 4	30 2	86 9
744	10	16	15	12	13	13							3 1	53 4	36 8	93 1
745	8	10	14	11	16								2 4	53 4	33 0	88 8
746	8	12	16	16	15								3 8	26 8	27 6	57 10
747	10	14	18	12	15	13							3 0	47 0	34 8	84 8
748	10	12	14	16	12	8							2 8	26 8	39 0	68 4
749	10	13	16	14	16	16							2 4	26 8	36 7	65 7
750	9	14	14	16	16	12							1 10	40 0	34 4	76 2
751	9	10	17	15	8	11							1 10	26 8	33 8	62 2
752	9	17	21	11	12	9–							3 1	66 8	23 4	93 1
753	8	12	13	16	15								2 0	40 0	24 10	66 10
754	8	13	16	10	14								2 4	40 0	30 0	72 4
755	8	8	11	17	16								2 1	26 8	28 9	57 6
756	10	16	21	17	16	12							2 6	53 4	26 6	82 4
757	9	13	16	19	11	8–							2 8	53 4	21 3	77 3
758	9	16	11	11	15	12							3 0	53 4	23 10	80 2
759	8	10	14	18	12								2 0	53 4	25 6	80 10
760	8–	13	14	15	13	8–							2 6	40 0	28 4	70 10
761	8	13	15	19	16	13							2 2	40 0	25 6	67 8
762	8	19	17	12	11								2 8	40 0	24 4	67 0
763	8	18	12	14	14								2 10	40 0	26 8	69 6
764	9	21	12	16	16	14							2 10	53 4	22 8	78 10
765	8	17	16	18	14								3 0	53 4	27 4	83 8
766	12	19	12	16	16	19	8						3 2	26 8	34 10	64 8
767	8	11	15	16	12								4 2	66 8	19 10	90 8
768	9	16	12	14	12	8–							3 2	26 8	31 8	61 6
769	10	14	16	15	15	10							3 1	45 0	28 6	76 7
770	9	16	16	12	14	14							3 4	53 4	30 6	87 2
771	8	12	12	10	16								2 3	26 8	28 4	57 3
772	8	14	12	15	15								2 4	40 0	26 10	69 2
773	11	17	19	15	17	13							3 3	26 8	45 7	75 6
774	8	16	8	16	16	12	15						2 8	26 8	41 6	70 10
775	8	18	14	15	15								3 2	53 4	27 6	84 0
776	9	16	19	12	16	10							3 1	26 8	39 0	68 9
777	8	19	22	16	13								2 10	53 4	26 8	82 10
778	8	16	12	18	14								2 6	26 8	36 10	66 0
779	9	14	19	16	12	16							2 4	26 8	38 4	67 4
780	10	16	16	11	18	13							2 6	26 8	31 3	61 5
781	9	18	14	12	12	10							3 1	26 8	30 0	59 9
782	8	18	20	11	13	5–							2 2	26 8	33 7	62 5

TABLE IV — (*Continued*).

SPECIMEN NUMBER.	Diameter of stump.	MEASUREMENTS ON STUMP. Number of rings per inch on stump, counting from the heart outward.																	Age in years.
783	1′ 0″	38	21	18	13	19	15												124
784	1 8	14	18	13	14	16	10	11	10	8									114
785	1 0	30	15	24	15	26	21												131
786	1 2	30	25	19	17	19	14	10											184
787	1 6	22	24	20	21	14	13	15	6	7	7								149
788	1 10	22	32	16	16	11	8	15	9	13	14	24							190
789	1 10	20	20	24	13	12	20	15	13	14	12	15	12						193
790	1 0	20	17	16	14	25	22												114
791	1 2	32	29	16	16	20	9	20	21										163
792	1 11	28	23	21	12	13	17	17	13	15	15	13	12						191
793	1 0	14	24	24	20	11	18	17											124
794	1 1	18	24	15	11	11	11	12											112
795	1 1	27	19	22	19	13	15	19	8-										143
796	1 2	25	18	16	18	11	16	9	8	9									130
797	1 3	32	33	22	18	12	14	9	8	6-									154
798	1 8	17	19	26	19	19	21	17	15	9	15	15	7-						199
799	1 8	18	23	17	24	18	12	12	12	9	14	15	16	18					208
800	1 6	28	16	18	19	17	13	12	13	12	7-								155
801	1 8	19	26	20	11	12	15	13	16	15	12	17	16						193
802	1 6	18	39	16	13	12	9	14	15	10	13	14	7-						180
803	1 8	35	32	29	12	11	14	8	9	10	8	14	11	20					213
804	1 1	42	40	30	25	17	18	19											171
805	1 8	22	20	13	21	18	14	14	9	17	18								166
806	1 5	23	24	16	19	15	14	16	16	18									164
807	1 1	18	24	27	23	22	24	22	18-										180
808	1 2	30	24	17	14	14	10	7	7										123
809	1 0	20	30	24	15	21	16												126
810	1 5	28	24	23	26	18	23	20	16	18	23	17							236
811	1 4	16	20	27	22	17	20	25	22	23	20								212
812	1 1	20	14	22	27	28	23	34											168
813	1 3	18	32	21	24	11	12	8	11										137
814	1 4	33	19	23	18	23	22	16	15	10	13-								192
815	1 4	14	28	17	13	12	14	16	9	6-									129
816	1 4	22	16	14	19	14	17	14	18	10-									144
817	1 6	14	18	18	15	18	13	16	16	20	20								163
818	1 5	14	18	17	22	23	17	17	16	19	10-								172
819	1 2	38	16	13	19	23	34	16											159
820	1 3	21	21	16	14	21	16	9	11	10									139
821	1 1	40	28	30	29	31	16	6-											175
822	2 0	33	30	22	10	8	7	12	10	12	18	14	11	10	9	8			218
823	1 5	32	18	18	31	22	21	18	14	18									198
824	1 0	34	23	18	17	20	24												136
825	1 6	19	19	25	27	30	14	15	14	10	14	15	7-						200
826	1 2	25	35	22	19	19	10	9											140
827	1 2	30	32	20	17	19	17	18	13										160
828	1 1	24	32	19	14	23	14	4-											130
829	1 2	23	26	24	23	18	22	22											158
830	1 1	37	27	23	23	19	22	11											162
831	1 6	30	22	23	18	20	16	14	17	28									188
832	2 2	23	13	21	20	12	11	15	13	12	7	21	13	10	6				197
833	1 8	19	26	27	20	17	13	11	19	18	19								189
834	1 2	26	18	25	19	15	14	13											180
835	1 0	33	26	35	24	18	15	7-											158
836	1 0	27	20	19	14	15	17												112
837	1 7	27	28	23	20	14	15	10	13	12	25								187
838	1 6	28	22	20	23	16	14	17	13	21	16								190
839	1 10	29	23	30	23	9	9	8	8	10	7	12	12						180
840	1 8	25	17	18	16	11	10	12	17	21	24								17
841	1 8	27	19	28	17	14	10	16	15	15	20	18							190
842	1 1	17	24	20	21	18	28	22-											150
843	1 4	30	30	25	17	16	15	17	10	18-									[illegible]
844	1 10	31	23	15	19	16	17	16	17	21	21	19							215
845	1 0	18	19	28	22	21	7												115
846	1 6	21	21	21	14	12	13	10	8	12	11	12							155
847	1 0	28	26	22	23	15	10												124
848	1 2	19	22	24	15	18	30	18	10										156
849	1 4	26	30	17	11	7	11	17	20	11	5-								165
850	1 3	23	33	21	18	18	18	16	12	11									175
851	1 3	22	19	13	16	15	17	16	18										136
852	1 2	16	21	28	22	20	22	20											149
853	1 2	26	25	28	19	28	24	26											176
854	1 4	28	23	28	33	12	14	8	11										157
855	1 0	28	17	17	16	14	30												124

Table IV — (*Continued*).

Specimen Number *Continued.*	Diameter of top in inches.	Top Measurements. Number of rings per inch at top, counting from the heart outward.											Height of stump.	Combined length of logs.	Length of top.	Total height.
783.....	8	12	17	14	15	....	....	....	....	....	....	....	2' 2"	26' 8"	32' 4"	61' 2"
784.....	8	14	17	14	15	....	....	....	....	....	....	....	3 2	40 0	26 6	69 8
785.....	8-	16	16	19	12	7-	....	....	....	....	....	....	2 4	26 8	34 8	63 8
786.....	9	16	18	17	17	12	....	....	....	....	....	....	2 8	26 8	31 4	60 8
787.....	8	18	12	10	19	6-	....	....	....	....	....	....	2 11	40 0	24 8	67 7
788.....	14	18	16	21	20	17	16	8	6-	....	....	....	3 2	40 0	40 4	83 6
789.....	9	10	14	19	11	10	....	....	....	....	....	....	4 0	53 4	34 3	91 7
790.....	8	12	14	14	15	....	....	....	....	....	....	....	2 0	26 8	31 10	60 6
791.....	8	16	15	15	17	....	....	....	....	....	....	....	2 6	40 0	24 0	66 6
792.....	14	18	17	15	14	12	16	8	....	....	....	....	3 8	40 0	38 4	82 0
793.....	8-	16	17	12	14	7-	....	....	....	....	....	....	4 2	26 8	34 8	65 6
794.....	9	12	18	14	16	10	....	....	....	....	....	....	3 2	26 8	33 6	63 4
795.....	8	14	16	16	17	....	....	....	....	....	....	....	3 0	40 0	24 6	67 6
796.....	8	16	12	20	8	6-	....	....	....	....	....	....	3 6	40 0	27 4	70 10
797.....	10	18	19	14	10	8	....	....	....	....	....	....	2 8	26 8	34 7	63 11
798.....	10	14	17	10	14	14	....	....	....	....	....	....	3 0	53 4	26 5	82 9
799.....	12	16	18	14	10	16	9	....	....	....	....	....	3 1	53 4	33 0	89 5
800.....	8-	14	12	17	15	10	....	....	....	....	....	....	3 3	53 4	27 6	84 1
801.....	10	16	16	14	15	12	....	....	....	....	....	....	4 0	53 4	26 10	84 2
802.....	10	14	11	16	14	10	....	....	....	....	....	....	3 8	40 0	36 0	79 8
803.....	9	16	9	13	12	7-	....	....	....	....	....	....	3 8	53 4	26 2	83 2
804.....	9	11	12	14	18	10	....	....	....	....	....	....	2 8	40 0	31 4	74 0
805.....	9	12	16	11	14	15	....	....	....	....	....	....	2 11	53 4	31 0	87 3
806.....	8	14	12	17	10	....	....	....	....	....	....	....	3 0	53 4	19 10	76 2
807.....	8	13	16	15	11	....	....	....	....	....	....	....	4 6	40 0	24 6	69 0
808.....	8	16	15	12	17	....	....	....	....	....	....	....	2 6	40 0	26 4	68 10
809.....	9	14	18	12	13	14	....	....	....	....	....	....	3 0	13 4	38 8	55 0
810.....	8	16	17	11	14	....	....	....	....	....	....	....	3 0	53 4	21 4	77 8
811.....	8-	15	14	11	10	12	....	....	....	....	....	....	3 4	53 4	24 4	81 0
812.....	8	16	17	12	9	6-	....	....	....	....	....	....	3 2	40 0	27 0	70 2
813.....	8	14	16	12	12	....	....	....	....	....	....	....	2 8	40 0	23 6	66 2
814.....	8	16	15	12	11	....	....	....	....	....	....	....	3 2	53 4	24 6	81 0
815.....	8	19	12	14	10	....	....	....	....	....	....	....	3 2	53 4	27 4	83 10
816.....	10	14	16	19	14	10	....	....	....	....	....	....	3 4	40 0	29 10	73 2
817.....	9	16	18	12	15	10	....	....	....	....	....	....	3 0	53 4	24 4	80 8
818.....	10	11	12	14	14	11	....	....	....	....	....	....	2 8	40 0	30 0	72 8
819.....	8	16	16	14	13	....	....	....	....	....	....	....	2 10	40 0	26 10	69 8
820.....	8	14	15	12	17	5-	....	....	....	....	....	....	2 10	40 0	24 4	67 2
821.....	8	18	20	12	14	....	....	....	....	....	....	....	2 6	26 8	31 6	60 8
822.....	14	13	18	15	14	13	15	17	14	....	....	....	3 0	40 0	42 7	85 7
823.....	9	13	14	16	12	12	....	....	....	....	....	....	2 10	53 4	27 4	83 6
824.....	8½	13	16	16	10	8-	....	....	....	....	....	....	2 10	26 8	32 6	62 0
825.....	8	14	13	15	15	6-	....	....	....	....	....	....	3 2	53 4	33 9	90 3
826.....	10	16	14	13	12	12	....	....	....	....	....	....	3 6	26 8	42 10	73 0
827.....	8	14	13	15	12	....	....	....	....	....	....	....	2 6	40 0	23 7	66 1
828.....	9	16	14	11	13	12	....	....	....	....	....	....	3 2	26 8	38 4	68 2
829.....	9	17	15	12	18	12	....	....	....	....	....	....	3 3	40 0	28 6	71 9
830.....	9	14	12	16	13	13	....	....	....	....	....	....	2 0	26 8	31 4	63 0
831.....	9	16	14	14	13	14	....	....	....	....	....	....	2 10	53 4	27 11	84 1
832.....	13	13	14	12	13	14	12	12	....	....	....	....	4 0	53 4	30 4	87 8
833.....	11	14	12	14	11	13	11	....	....	....	....	....	3 4	53 4	32 8	89 4
834.....	8	16	12	11	15	....	....	....	....	....	....	....	3 0	40 0	28 4	71 4
835.....	8-	14	13	11	14	10	....	....	....	....	....	....	2 5	26 8	30 0	59 1
836.....	8	15	12	14	18	....	....	....	....	....	....	....	2 8	26 8	31 4	60 8
837.....	11	14	15	11	13	13	....	....	....	....	....	....	3 0	40 0	38 7	81 7
838.....	10	13	12	16	14	10	....	....	....	....	....	....	3 2	40 0	37 4	80 6
839.....	8	13	14	12	14	....	....	....	....	....	....	....	4 0	66 8	27 10	98 6
840.....	10	14	13	11	12	12	....	....	....	....	....	....	3 8	53 4	31 8	88 8
841.....	10	16	14	14	13	15	....	....	....	....	....	....	2 10	40 0	36 4	79 2
842.....	8	16	12	2	17	....	....	....	....	....	....	....	2 8	40 0	26 6	69 2
843.....	9	14	13	15	16	12	....	....	....	....	....	....	3 4	53 4	28 10	85 6
844.....	9	16	14	12	13	12	....	....	....	....	....	....	3 1	66 8	21 3	91 0
845.....	8	16	13	12	14	....	....	....	....	....	....	....	2 8	26 8	31 5	60 9
846.....	10	14	15	11	16	12	....	....	....	....	....	....	2 10	40 0	33 7	76 5
847.....	8	14	15	12	16	....	....	....	....	....	....	....	2 8	26 8	34 3	63 7
848.....	9	16	15	13	13	8	....	....	....	....	....	....	3 0	40 0	31 6	74 6
849.....	8	12	14	17	10	6-	....	....	....	....	....	....	2 10	53 4	27 6	83 8
850.....	8	12	16	14	11	....	....	....	....	....	....	....	2 8	40 0	26 10	69 6
851.....	10	14	18	12	13	10	....	....	....	....	....	....	3 2	26 8	43 4	73 2
852.....	8	16	14	15	12	6-	....	....	....	....	....	....	3 1	40 0	26 7	69 8
853.....	8	14	14	16	19	....	....	....	....	....	....	....	2 10	53 4	36 8	92 10
854.....	10	13	17	15	12	14	....	....	....	....	....	....	2 8	26 8	42 4	71 8
855.....	10	14	16	15	11	11	....	....	....	....	....	....	2 4	13 4	41 10	60 6

7

TABLE IV — (*Continued*).

SPECIMEN NUMBER.	Diameter of stump.	MEASUREMENTS ON STUMP. Number of rings per inch on stump, counting from the heart outward.																	Age in years.
856	1' 6"	20	22	11	14	14	14	16	12	18	17								159
857	1 7	17	9	6	10	6	6	17	6	7	5	6-							95
858	1 2	27	26	19	20	18	17	25											152
859	1 2	22	24	30	20	15	11	20	16										158
860	1 1	22	23	30	23	22	18	25											168
861	1 5	20	24	24	18	13	11	7	6	8									131
862	1 0	24	28	24	15	16	15	14											136
863	1 0	22	23	21	16	14	16												113
864	1 3	20	15	17	20	10	19	17	14										132
865	1 1	36	23	15	17	6	14	15-											136
866	1 2	18	18	30	21	17	17	24	18-										163
867	1 8	30	29	26	18	23	16	16	11	16	15								200
868	1 0	35	30	32	25	10	9												141
869	1 4	25	20	16	15	17	14	14	16										137
870	1 8	25	27	20	15	12	12	13	14	10	16	12-							176
871	1 8	22	30	24	16	18	16	15	9	12	15	21							198
872	1 2	24	29	18	15	16	15	23	19										179
873	1 0	30	15	16	21	16	14												112
874	1 2	25	13	13	12	14	10	17	8-										110
875	1 1	17	19	23	14	14	11	10											107
876	1 2	29	17	16	13	10	9	8	4-										106
877	1 1	20	19	24	19	9	10	8											109
878	1 8	28	34	19	16	11	13	8	13	9	7	6-							164
879	1 1	36	25	13	18	15	8	11											128
880	1 6	24	22	14	15	18	15	7	7	11									133
881	1 2	26	27	15	11	13	8	11											111
882	1 1	30	17	18	15	7	8	9	10										114
883	1 2	28	35	22	11	7	8	8											119
884	1 5	30	26	29	20	11	12	13	8	16									164
885	1 2	26	21	17	11	14	6	9	14										118
886	1 0	22	29	21	15	11	18												115
887	1 1	30	28	20	18	14	20	12-											142
888	1 0	20	13	12	12	14	16	9-											96
889	1 4	30	26	16	16	8	13	15	14	16	15								160
890	1 6	29	22	19	21	15	11	8	11	13	10-								150
891	1 0	20	22	22	15	17	29												118
892	1 4	20	24	24	29	23	22	19	7-										167
893	1 1	30	28	16	13	10	6	5	9										117
894	1 4	25	30	20	17	7	9	8											116
895	1 1	26	44	22	14	7	6	7											126
896	1 0	24	28	22	16	14	15	8-											127
897	1 0	20	24	28	22	24	30												148
898	1 5	28	24	24	20	20	15	12	19	16									178
899	1 3	24	20	17	16	13	17	8	8	10									133
900	1 8	21	28	20	12	10	10	8	11	9	13	14							156
901	1 0	22	14	16	18	24	8	12-											124
902	1 0	28	34	16	9	12	13												112
903	1 3	23	28	24	12	13	14	10	15	17									156
904	1 7	18	16	15	15	14	17	16	19	24									164
905	1 5	19	24	19	12	13	13	15	14	21									150
906	1 0	22	24	24	24	30	27												151
907	1 0	16	15	16	17	16	21												101
908	1 1	19	22	20	23	19	10	14											127
909	1 8	18	20	22	32	24	14	8	11	10	31								190
910	1 0	26	28	12	17	24	27												134
911	1 7	24	25	23	30	21	15	14	18	14	6-								191
912	1 6	27	30	24	27	22	7	11	10	18	15								191
913	1 8	19	16	13	23	30	17	14	16	14	25								186
914	1 2	25	26	22	20	22	20	19	14										163
915	1 0	32	21	16	20	16	14	6											125
916	1 2	24	30	23	14	10	13	18	10-										147
917	1 2	16	24	30	21	15	16	6											138
918	1 6	26	26	17	22	18	14	7	13	13	14	7-							177
919	1 5	22	20	27	14	17	10	20	9										139
920	1 8	19	26	25	15	10	14	12	13	16	18								163
921	1 2	22	24	22	15	24	23	23	4-										150
922	1 2	26	30	24	12	11	13	14	18	11									159
923	1 5	30	33	22	13	17	11	9	18	26									179
924	1 0	24	24	21	18	16	12	5-											120
925	1 2	20	21	18	22	24	14	22	8-										152
926	1 1	18	21	14	9	14	11	11	6-										104
927	1 2	20	18	19	15	16	14	16	8-										126
928	1 2	18	24	22	14	16	14	12	10	6-									136

Table IV — (*Continued*).

Specimen Number *Continued.*	Diameter of top in inches.	Top Measurements. Number of rings per inch at top, counting from the heart outward.											Height of stump.	Combined length of logs.	Length of top.	Total height.
856.....	9	14	15	12	12	16	....	....	....	....	....	....	3′ 4″	53′ 4″	28′ 3″	84′ 11
857.....	8	14	10	11	12	....	....	....	....	....	....	....	3 6	66 8	22 7	92 9
858.....	9	14	16	13	10	11	....	....	....	....	....	....	3 4	40 0	27 6	70 10
859.....	8	16	15	12	13	.	....	....	....	....	....	....	3 6	53 4	26 5	83 3
860.....	9	12	13	17	14	10	....	....	....	....	....	....	3 2	26 8	33 8	63 6
861.....	8	14	13	12	14	..	....	....	....	....	....	....	2 8	53 4	22 4	78 4
862.....	8	16	12	15	11	....	....	....	....	....	....	....	3 0	26 8	36 0	65 8
863.....	8	14	16	10	13	.	....	....	....	....	....	....	2 0	26 8	32 6	61 2
864.....	8	10	16	16	12	6-	....	....	....	....	....	....	2 8	40 0	36 11	79 7
865.....	9	9	11	17	12	14	....	....	....	....	....	....	2 6	40 0	34 9	77 3
866.....	10	12	11	12	16	19	....	....	....	....	....	....	2 8	26 8	45 4	74 8
867.....	9	12	16	17	10	10	....	....	....	....	....	....	3 0	53 4	32 10	89 2
868.....	8	16	11	14	10	5-	..	....	....	....	....	....	2 2	26 8	34 7	63 5
869.....	12	10	16	11		....	....	....	....	....	....	....	3 4	26 8	33 0	63 0
870.....	10	14	17	8	11	11	....	....	....	....	....	....	3 2	53 4	31 4	87 10
871.....	9	16	14	12	12	10	....	....	....	...	....	....	3 0	66 8	26 10	96 6
872.....	9	14	15	10	17	12	....	....	....	....	....	....	2 10	40 0	34 3	77 1
873.....	8	16	12	11	14	7-	....	....	....	....	....	....	2 7	26 8	42 8	71 11
874.....	10	12	13	10	17	15	....	....	....	....	....	....	2 5	26 8	34 11	64 0
875.....	8	14	14	14	9	....	....	....	....	....	....	....	2 6	26 8	37 3	66 5
876.....	8	16	12	11	8	...	....	....	....	....	....	....	2 8	26 8	34 8	64 0
877.....	8-	14	17	13	10	7-	....	....	....	....	....	....	3 4	26 8	32 5	62 5
878.....	10	16	12	12	17	11	..	....	....	....	....	....	2 11	40 0	26 10	69 9
879.....	9	14	19	12	15	10	....	....	....	....	....	....	2 2	26 8	31 6	60 4
880.....	8	10	16	10	18	....	....	....	....	....	....	....	2 10	40 0	30 8	73 6
881.....	8	14	12	12	11	....	....	....	....	...	....	....	2 8	26 8	27 4	56 8
882.....	8	16	14	10	9	....	....	..	....	....	....	....	2 4	26 8	26 0	55 0
883.....	8-	6	12	11	11	10	....	....	....	....	....	....	3 1	26 8	27 6	57 3
884.....	10	16	16	12	13	9	....	....	....	....	....	....	2 10	40 0	24 7	67 5
885.....	9	14	11	15	10	12	....	....	....	....	....	....	2 3	40 0	26 0	68 3
886.....	7-	12	14	9	11	...	....	....	....	....	....	....	2 1	26 8	27 0	55 9
887.....	9	16	16	10	12	17	....	....	....	....	..	....	2 3	40 0	29 3	71 6
888.....	8	11	12	18	10	....	....	....	....	....	....	....	1 11	26 8	39 6	68 1
889.....	9	17	11	10	14	12	....	....	....	....	....	....	4 0	53 4	25 8	83 0
890.....	10	14	16	10	10	17	....	....	....	....	....	....	3 10	53 4	27 6	84 8
891.....	8-	14	11	15	16	....	....	....	....	....	....	....	2 4	13 4	45 10	61 6
892.....	9	12	19	11	14	10	....	....	....	....	....	....	2 4	40 0	28 6	70 10
893.....	8	16	12	13	14	....	....	....	....	....	...	...	2 2	26 8	27 4	56 2
894.....	8-	14	14	7	13	7-	....	....	....	....	....	....	2 4	26 8	29 3	58 3
895.....	8	18	12	14	10	....	....	....	....	....	....	....	2 6	26 8	21 8	50 10
896.....	9	16	14	15	10	11	....	....	....	....	....	....	2 2	13 4	42 10	58 4
897.....	8	14	17	17	14	....	....	....	....	....	....	....	2 2	26 8	31 4	60 2
898.....	12	16	16	18	12	14	14	7-	....	....	....	....	3 0	26 8	43 8	73 4
899.....	8	19	12	12	14	.	....	....	....	....	....	....	2 8	53 4	24 3	80 3
900.....	10	19	10	17	12	10	....	....	....	....	....	....	3 1	66 8	21 10	91 7
901.....	8	14	14	13	9	....	....	....	....	....	....	....	2 4	26 8	41 2	70 2
902.....	7-	16	11	14	16	....	....	....	....	....	....	...	2 4	26 8	34 10	63 10
903.....	9	12	14	14	17	10	....	....	....	....	....	..	2 6	40 0	33 0	75 6
904.....	9	13	14	14	12	16	....	....	....	....	....	....	2 8	53 4	27 0	83 0
905.....	10	11	12	10	9	15	....	....	....	....	...	....	3 0	40 0	33 7	76 7
906.....	8	14	16	12	14	....	....	....	....	....	....	....	1 10	26 8	31 2	59 8
907.....	9-	12	14	15	12	12	....	....	....	....	....	....	2 0	26 8	36 0	64 8
908.....	9-	13	13	2	14	12	....	....	....	....		....	2 4	40 0	21 6	63 10
909.....	8	12	14	9	10	6-	....	....	....	....	....	....	3 0	66 8	19 10	89 6
910.....	10	16	15	8	9	11	....	....	....	....	....	....	2 8	26 8	30 0	59 4
911.....	9	16	12	12	10	9	....	....	....	....	....	..	3 0	53 4	22 6	78 10
912.....	9	14	11	8	13	10	....	....	....	....	....	....	3 2	53 4	21 4	77 10
913.....	10	12	13	14	14	9	....	....	....	....	....	....	3 0	53 4	30 8	87 0
914.....	9	13	16	12	16	10	....	....	..	....	....	..	4 2	40 0	34 11	79 1
915.....	8	14	16	12	13	....	....	....	....	....	....	....	3 0	40 0	29 7	72 7
916.....	9	16	11	13	13	10	....	..	....	....	....	....	3 2	31 8	29 0	76 10
917.....	8	14	12	14	14	....	....	....	....	....	....	..	4 4	53 4	22 10	80 6
918.....	13	4	12	13	11	13	10	6-	....	....	....	....	4 1	40 0	42 4	86 5
919.....	9	14	12	13	12	11	....	....	...	....	....	....	3 10	53 4	31 8	88 10
920.....	10	13	16	12	12	13	....	....	....	....	....	....	4 2	53 4	29 8	87 2
921.....	10	16	13	14	12	12	....	....	....	....	....	..	4 0	26 8	41 6	72 2
922.....	9	12	14	14	13	10		....	....	....	...	....	4 2	40 0	34 10	79 0
923.....	10	14	11	11	6	15	6-	....	....	....	...	....	4 4	40 0	43 0	87 4
924.....	9	12	13	13	16	16	....	....	....	....	....	....	4 0	26 8	43 6	74 2
925.....	9½	13	12	14	15	12	....	....	....	....	....	....	3 10	26 8	40 8	71 2
926.....	8	12	13	14	10	....	....	....	....	....	....	....	2 8	40 0	32 7	75 3
927.....	10	14	14	11	10	9	....	....	....	....	....	....	2 6	26 8	42 6	71 8
928.....	8	15	13	11	14	....	....	....	....	....	....	....	2 10	40 0	29 8	72 6

TABLE IV — (*Concluded*).

SPECIMEN NUMBER.	Diameter of stump.	MEASUREMENTS ON STUMP. Number of rings per inch on stump, counting from the heart outward.																	Age in years.
929	1' 2"	18	22	27	23	13	17	18	18										156
930	1 4	22	28	22	19	17	17	13	23										160
931	1 2	23	16	24	22	21	20	18											159
932	1 5	22	24	25	25	22	18	14	22	12-									184
933	1 0	23	26	22	18	10	18												127
934	1 1	22	25	30	17	18	20	9											141
935	1 2	14	16	18	10	12	11	13	10										104
936	1 2	19	24	28	20	13	17	20	8										149
937	1 0	18	24	24	16	16	36												134
938	1 0	25	26	19	20	12	28												130
939	1 4	24	30	24	26	19	17	20	17	5-									182
940	1 4	28	34	28	22	25	19	22											178
941	1 5	28	24	14	16	16	16	16	10	12									152
942	1 4	21	26	24	18	22	16	21	12	6-									166
943	1 2	17	22	22	20	23	26	11											140
944	1 6	29	30	26	21	22	22	15	8	11	6-								189
945	1 6	20	19	18	25	18	15	14	12	18	11-								170
946	1 8	21	22	22	21	12	18	14	13	12	14	28							211
947	1 1	22	26	28	24	24	20	9-											153
948	1 6	24	20	19	18	19	19	18	16	19	28								200
949	1 2	17	22	26	25	24	16	17	7-										154
950	1 8	21	23	30	28	26	18	18	9	18	17	12							221
951	1 4	26	36	23	16	11	18	17	13										160
952	1 1	24	26	22	18	20	18	15											143
953	1 6	28	30	20	16	14	18	14	13	9									172
954	1 8	18	20	20	18	14	18	11	15	18	21	12							185
955	1 1	23	16	20	24	20	17	7-											127
956	1 1	21	16	24	22	17	21	16											140
957	1 2	18	24	28	28	18	23	19											158
958	1 1	28	30	26	17	15	14	15											145
959	1 2	24	20	19	18	16	14	15	8-										134
960	1 2	18	19	20	22	22	20	14	4-										139
961	1 3	30	34	10	18	13	10	13	9-										146
962	1 3	36	30	15	15	11	15	18	31										170
963	1 3	34	38	22	17	18	13	20	13										175
964	1 8	24	22	25	26	25	16	12	12	18	16								196
965	2 0	30	29	34	17	14	12	10	9	10	12	14	18						209
966	1 2	36	20	32	28	26	14	18	10-										184
967	1 4	26	28	18	20	15	15	16	20										158
968	1 0	30	24	21	21	19	15	8-											138
969	1 8	22	36	23	11	12	12	8	13	17	14								171
970	1 5	36	42	29	23	14	10	11	12	12	7-								196
971	1 0	36	42	38	19	17	15												167
972	1 0	24	18	28	27	14	12												183
973	1 1	28	29	15	21	13	10	4											120
974	1 0	21	26	24	19	13	8												111
975	1 2	24	25	14	13	8	15	12	11										122
976	1 2	22	17	14	21	20	13	19	9-										135
977	1 0	20	19	23	21	20	20	10-											133
978	1 2	30	20	17	16	14	18	9											124
979	1 1	18	14	18	12	18	14	20											114
980	1 0	18	17	16	15	20	15	6-											107
981	1 1	28	18	16	16	13	14	17	22										144
982	1 4	21	27	20	21	17	18	16	18										158
983	1 6	25	25	21	22	16	14	14	16	10	9								176
984	1 1	32	24	18	16	18	5	14	10										147
985	1 4	21	20	20	18	17	22	14	18										150
986	1 8	23	26	24	16	14	16	15	20	17	15								186
987	1 6	24	23	24	12	13	13	9	12	10	9								148
988	1 0	22	28	22	16	15	20												123
989	1 1	26	28	29	16	20	16	13											147
990	1 0	30	28	24	18	17	15												182
991	1 2	18	22	22	24	14	16	17											133
992	1 6	21	20	25	16	13	7	8	11	13	11								148
993	1 0	28	24	15	15	14	15	8-											114
994	1 0	22	23	11	17	12	10												95
995	1 1	29	30	31	22	17	18	26											173
996	1 6	25	28	24	18	14	23	14	15	13	26								2 0
997	1 0	29	20	22	20	18	28												184
998	1 2	26	25	18	18	24	20	13	10										154
999	1 1	24	28	21	21	11	8	8	13	17									148
1000	1 2	32	29	31	23	13	14	8	4-										154

TABLE IV — (*Concluded*).

SPECIMEN NUMBER *Continued.*	Diameter of top in inches.	Top Measurements. Number of rings per inch at top, counting from the heart outward.											Height of stump.	Combined length of logs.	Length of top.	Total height.
929....	9	13	14	10	10	9							2′ 8″	40′ 0″	28′ 10″	71′ 6″
930....	11	12	12	14	9	8	9						3 0	53 4	29 11	86 3
931....	8	12	11	10	10								3 1	40 0	26 4	69 5
932....	8	14	13	13	11								3 4	53 4	22 6	79 2
933....	8	11	13	12	12								3 0	16 8	32 7	62 3
934....	9	10	11	13	11	10							4 4	26 8	44 7	75 7
935....	10	14	11	10	10	14							3 2	40 0	33 8	76 10
936....	8	14	14	14	9								2 10	40 0	31 2	74 0
937....	8	13	13	16	14								2 2	26 8	36 7	65 5
938....	8	13	14	15	14								2 4	40 0	26 10	69 2
939....	8	14	16	16	12								3 2	66 8	21 7	91 5
940....	11	12	13	16	14	11							3 1	40 0	29 10	72 11
941....	8	12	14	14	12								2 10	53 4	22 4	78 6
942....	11	12	12	13	14	16	8–						3 4	40 0	33 6	76 10
943....	9	14	14	14	12	10							3 0	40 0	31 4	74 4
944....	9	14	10	13	13	11							3 0	40 0	31 0	74 0
945....	11	14	16	14	15	10	10						2 6	40 0	30 4	72 10
946....	12	14	16	14	13	12	12	14					2 10	26 8	49 10	79 4
947....	8–	16	12	10	11	12							2 10	26 8	31 4	60 10
948....	9	14	14	11	13	16							3 6	40 0	28 4	71 10
949....	9	18	12	13	13	10							3 2	40 0	26 10	70 0
950....	10	14	12	12	5	11							3 2	53 4	27 9	84 3
951....	13	16	4	14	16	10	11	8–					2 10	13 4	50 4	66 6
952....	9	12	16	11	12	9							4 0	26 8	28 6	59 2
953....	10	12	16	12	13	11							4 0	53 4	26 4	83 8
954....	10	14	12	14	13	10							3 6	53 4	19 6	76 4
955....	8	14	16	12	10								3 10	26 8	33 2	63 8
956....	8	16	17	9	11								3 4	26 8	30 10	60 10
957....	10	17	19	11	10	9							3 6	26 8	38 3	68 5
958....	8	12	12	14	14								3 2	26 8	33 4	63 2
959....	9	18	11	13	12								2 7	40 0	26 8	69 3
960....	8½	11	14	14	12	12							2 8	40 0	24 10	67 6
961....	8–	14	15	15	10	12							2 10	40 0	29 3	72 1
962....	11	6	9	14	16	15	18						2 6	26 8	42 7	71 9
963....	9	13	11	11	17	14							2 8	40 0	30 3	73 11
964....	12	7	8	10	16	17	19						3 0	40 0	28 11	71 11
965....	10	14	16	12	19	11							3 0	53 4	28 7	84 11
966....	8	12	12	17	11								2 4	40 0	19 10	62 2
967....	8	14	16	11	9	6–							2 10	40 0	26 4	69 2
968....	8	19	14	10	8								2 8	26 8	25 0	54 4
969....	10	9	21	17	12	8							3 0	53 4	21 10	78 2
970....	9½	16	19	11	13	7–							3 0	40 0	32 6	75 6
971....	9	10	18	17	11	11							3 1	26 8	35 7	65 4
972....	8	9	7	12	15								2 4	26 8	30 0	59 0
973....	8½	12	16	16	11	8							2 6	26 8	26 9	55 11
974....	9	17	20	13	14	8							2 0	13 4	42 3	57 7
975....	9½	12	19	16	10	10							2 2	26 8	36 10	65 8
976....	9	16	11	15	16	8							2 4	26 8	39 0	68 0
977....	8	14	13	17	11								1 10	40 0	31 2	73 0
978....	8½	14	11	18	13	6–							2 4	26 8	36 10	65 10
979....	8	16	11	15	12								2 0	26 8	38 6	67 2
980....	8	16	11	13	14								1 11	26 8	24 9	63 4
981....	8	14	12	18	10								2 2	26 8	33 6	62 4
982....	9	16	12	19	18	11							2 8	40 0	29 4	72 0
983....	12	21	17	13	14	18	8						2 9	40 0	40 2	82 11
984....	9	19	18	11	16	12							2 4	26 8	30 0	59 0
985....	10	20	14	19	11	10							2 3	40 0	28 6	70 9
986....	12	19	19	12	14	14	10						2 10	40 0	38 3	81 1
987....	8½	16	16	10	15	12							2 6	40 0	34 4	76 10
988....	8	11	19	12	14								1 4	16 8	31 6	59 6
989....	8	14	16	15	12								3 0	26 8	40 4	70 0
990....	8	12	19	13	13								2 10	26 8	23 0	52 6
991....	10	14	16	12	13	14							2 8	26 8	26 10	56 2
992....	8	14	14	19	10								2 9	40 0	27 6	70 3
993....	8	16	12	17	11								1 11	26 8	31 8	60 [illegible]
994....	8	14	13	19	8								2 2	13 4	36 0	51 6
995....	9	19	18	14	10								2 4	26 8	34 10	63 10
996....	10	19	21	20	11	11							2 6	40 0	28 6	71 0
997....	9	23	19	17	8								2 0	13 4	52 2	67 6
998....	8	11	17	16	12								2 3	40 0	24 6	66 9
999....	8	12	19	17	14								2 1	26 8	31 4	60 1
1000....	9	16	12	19	20	16							2 0	26 8	38 2	66 10

In connection with the preceding tables it may be stated that all of the 700 trees first examined were found on Township 20, Franklin county, between two large ponds, Floodwood and Long Pond. The two main slopes on this land run north and south, with little or no difference in the timber on either slope. This township has an average elevation of about 1,600 feet above the sea. The spruce was above the average in quantity per acre, and in quality it was first class. The trees were thrifty, but few being found that were rotten at the stump. Not a tree had died within the past ten years, the absence of any dead spruce having been noted by the foresters. In size the trees were above the average diameter for Adirondack black spruce.

On Township 20, in a few places where the spruce was standing in "clumps," there was a yield of 40 standard logs (8,000 feet, B. M.) per acre; where it was scattered through the other timber, 15 standards (3,000 feet) would be a fair average.

On Lots 34 and 35, Township 3, St. Lawrence county, the spruce growing in clumps measured, in two different places, 35 standard logs (7,000 feet) to the acre. Where it was scattered among other species, it measured 12 standards per acre on an average.

On Lots 50 and 63, Township 3, St. Lawrence county, the spruce did not grow in clumps at all, but averaged 15 standard logs to the acre.

The spruce in each case was growing either in small clumps or was scattered among hardwoods composed of beech, hard maple, and yellow birch, the beech predominating in number of trees, although of inferior diameter and height. The black spruce overtops the hardwoods where its diameter exceeds 14 inches; when standing in clumps it is taller than the scattered spruces of the same diameter growing among the hardwoods. Where it grows in clumps the spruce has a small crown, the limbs being small and short; but in a scattering growth the spruces, as soon as they overtop surrounding hardwoods, put out their limbs thickly and large.

A spruce 20 inches in diameter growing in a clump of spruces will yield five logs, 13 feet 4 inches in length, while one of the same diameter in a scattered growth mixed with hardwoods will yield but four logs. In the one growing among hardwoods, after four logs

SAWING FALLEN TREES INTO LOGS.

G. H. Elson, Photo.

have been cut from its trunk, the diameter of the last or top log at its small end will be from 10 to 12 inches, but the limbs above this point will be so thick and large that the fifth log would not be over five or six inches at the top, and would not be accepted by the lumbermen. A tree of the same species and size growing in a clump will yield five logs, because the shaft does not diminish in size so fast owing to the lighter growth of limbs that form its top. While the largest spruces are found scattered among the hardwoods, the tallest ones of like diameters are found growing in the spruce clumps.

A coarse, gravelly soil, with a southern or western slope, seems most favorable for the best development of this species. Before the axemen came into this locality there was an ample growth of young spruces or nurslings thickly scattered throughout the timber; but where the spruce grew thickly, the felling of trees scarred and broke down most of the nurslings. Where the spruce was scattered through the hardwoods the young trees did not suffer so much from the careless felling of the axemen.

The spruce blight of twenty years ago did not make its appearance in Township 20, on which the first 700 trees examined were growing. In fact, this locality is remarkable for its exemption from injury in that respect.

There are but few balsams (*Abies balsamea*) growing among the spruces which furnished the specimens examined by the foresters, although many trees of this species are growing along the edges or shores of neighboring swamps and ponds. The balsam in this vicinity is small, ranging from three to seven inches in diameter near the ground. It is very scarce, however, in the vicinity of this spruce growth, there being many acres on which no balsam is found; neither was there any cedar. There are a few tamaracks (*Larix Americana*) on these lots, but they are all dead, having succumbed to the attacks of the sawfly (*Nematus Erichsonii*) which within a few years has destroyed all the tamarack in the Adirondacks. But little white pine was found among the spruce where these measurements were taken. On the north shore of East Pine Pond, there was a piece of timber composed almost wholly of that species,—nice, thrifty, sound timber of large size. The owner, Mr. Snell, said that he cut 1,000 standards (200,000 feet, B. M.) of white pine logs on less than ten acres of land near the west end of East Pine Pond. There were a few black ash trees scattered throughout the timber where the spruce was growing, but no cherry.

In Township 3, St. Lawrence county, a few elms were growing among the spruces and hardwoods, a species rarely seen in the Adirondack forest.

A noticeable feature in the growth of the black spruce is that the annual accretion of wood in the trunk is not concentric, the total growth being considerably greater on one side of the heart than on the opposite side. The extent of this eccentricity is apparent in some of the figures given in Table IV, in which the diameter of each tree is not only given, but the number of inches and growth per inch of the longest radius. For instance, Specimen No. 1 had a diameter of 18 inches on the stump, but the figures showing the number of annual rings for each inch in growth indicate that instead of nine inches, which would have been one-half the diameter, there were eleven inches between the heart and the bark. Specimen No. 77 is fourteen inches in diameter, but the heart is nine inches from the bark. Specimen No. 135, with a diameter of thirteen inches, shows that there were nine inches between the bark and the heart. In Specimen 237 it will be seen that the heart was two inches nearer one side of the tree than the other. In No. 383 the radius is 17 instead of 12 inches. This lack of concentricity, as measured by the abnormal length of the longest radius, varies from one to five inches.

A remarkable feature of this one-sided growth is that it is mostly in one direction. The foresters who examined the trees in Township 20 were instructed to note carefully the compass point to which in each case the longest radius of tree growth pointed. Of 700 trees examined in Township 20, Franklin county, (the first 700 specimens in Table IV,) this abnormal or one-sided growth was directed as follows:

Direction.	Trees.
North	471
Northeast	81
East	106
South	1
West	27
Southwest	6
Northwest	8
	700

There seems to be no satisfactory explanation of this tendency of the black spruce to a one-sided growth. After careful observations in search of some reason, no regular conditions of slope, exposure or environment were found upon which to base any theory. It has been asserted frequently, however, that this uneven growth on either side of the heart was due to an uneven distribution of the roots; and that the greater accretion in the tree trunk would be found on the side of the tree on which lay the largest roots.

In the preceding tables the indicated age of the tree is based upon the number of rings revealed by the stump; but in each case if the tree had been cut close to the ground a greater number of rings would have been found and consequently a greater age indicated. This should be borne in mind in connection with the statistics referred to. The stumps varied in height from one to four feet, the height of the stump depending in each case upon the convenience of the axeman and the position in which he stood while at work.

One column of figures in Table IV indicates the length of the section taken by the lumbermen for their logs, and represents one, two, or three logs of 13 feet 4 inches each, that being the length cut by the log-choppers in the Adirondack forests. For instance; in Specimen No. 6 (right-hand page), 26 feet and 8 inches of trunk were taken, showing that two logs were obtained from that tree. Specimen 19 shows that a section of the trunk 40 feet long was removed, from which it appears that this tree furnished three logs; and specimen 60, that 53 feet and 4 inches of the tree trunk, making four logs, were taken. Specimen 83 shows that five logs aggregating 66 feet and 8 inches were taken, the top log being only eight inches in diameter at the top or small end. In this tree it appears, from the next column of figures, that only 15 feet and 5 inches of top remained, indicating that this tree, which was 84 feet 9 inches high, was not only tall, but cylindrical and free from limbs nearly to its crown. Specimen 87 was 93 feet and 7 inches high, and although taller than the one just mentioned, furnished the same number of logs, the top log, however, being 12 inches in diameter at its small end.

The tallest tree mentioned in Table IV is Specimen 839, which was 98 feet 6 inches high, and 22 inches in diameter on the stump. Specimen 832 was 26 inches in diameter, but only 87 feet 8 inches high, and furnished four logs instead of five. It will be noticed that many of the trees furnished only two logs and some only one, although they were of a fair height. The small number of logs obtained from a tree was due in some instances to rotten butts, or to the fact that there was too great a limb development at the top of the tree, the top measurements indicating in many cases that the trunk diminished in diameter, or "tapered" too rapidly.

In Table IV the figures showing the number of rings per inch indicate that the Adirondack black spruce when growing under natural conditions, where the trees are overcrowded and deprived of light, requires on an average over 24 years for an increase of two inches in diameter; but an examination of the figures shows that many of the trees, which had attained a height enabling them to dominate the surrounding ones, required from six to eight years only to gain two inches. Thus the tree represented by Specimen 43 was 30 years in gaining the third inch of radius while it was only seven years in growing an inch after its crown had reached to where it could gain proper nourishment. Specimen 456 evidently had the advantage of light and air from the time that it was a nursling, as is indicated by the comparatively small number of years required in adding each inch to its diameter.

From the measurements and notes made by Forester Humes — in Township 14, Town of Fine, St. Lawrence county — the following deductions as to the average age of the spruce are made:

TABLE V.

DIAMETER IN INCHES.	Number of trees.*	Maximum and minimum ages.	Average age.
13	10	138—200	173
14	9	145—275	181
15	4	174—203	184
16	5	167—201	183
17	6	156—200	183
18	4	173—200	184
19	23	184—283	211
20	15	189—289	212
21	15	199—291	246
22	19	107—345	248
23	16	189—300	266
24	19	178—301	270
25	29	195—302	270
26	15	231—354	285
27	18	258—316	288
28	7	271—301	281
29	7	273—333	304
30	5	2[illegible]5—325	299
31	4	231—293	272
32	1	290—...	290
33	1	285—...	285
34	3	302—374	330
36	2	326—351	338
	237		

* These trees do not represent any definite area or yield per acre, but were selected with reference to securing specimens of each diameter.

And from the measurements and notes made by Foresters Olmstead and Sanford in Township 20, Franklin county, and Township 3 ("Atherton"), St Lawrence county, the following deductions as to the average age of the Adirondack spruce are made:

TABLE VI.

DIAMETER IN INCHES.	Number of spruce trees.	Minimum and maximum ages.	Average age.
12	217	96—185	128
13	177	102 · 210	139
14	187	104—214	143
15	71	114 – 217	151
16	113	116—212	154
17	53	121—236	161
18	77	130—209	154
19	17	95—200	174
20	53	133—235	184
21	4	156—227	185
22	12	162—224	189
23	4	149—234	186
24	10	160—226	195
25	1	213—...	213
26	1	197—...	197
27	3	217—226	222
	1,000		

We are unable to account satisfactorily for the difference in average age as indicated in the two preceding tables. It may be that if the figures in the first had included as large a number of trees and as wide a scope of territory as are embraced in the second table, that the two results would agree better. The average age as indicated in Table V corresponds substantially with that of the black spruce in Maine, as based upon measurements made by Mr. Austin Cary, whose report shows that the average age of the 12-inch spruce is 171 years; the 13-inch, 174 years; the 14-inch, 189 years, and the 15-inch, 185 years.

A remarkable feature in connection with the biology of the spruce is the exceedingly wide range of ages in trees of the same diameter. Thus, in Table VI it will be noted that of 187 trees all 14 inches in diameter on the stump, there is a difference of 110 years in some of the ages. Some will readily explain this

G. H. Elson, Photo.

wide divergence by claiming that in many cases there were two or more rings formed in single years owing to climatic effects, which is discussed later on.

But, in view of the short season in the Adirondacks during which the flow of sap is not checked, as might occur in trees which feel the influence of an early spring, only one ring could reasonably be expected for each year's growth. It is more reasonable to account for the rapid growth of some of the trees by the fact that these trees stood where they received more light and air; and for the slow growth of the others by the deprivation of the same.

Although the black spruce is the slowest in growth of all our forest trees, it does not require the number of years to attain maturity that are indicated by the preceding statistics. It must be borne in mind that these tables indicate the age of the spruce when growing under natural conditions, where it is deprived of a proper amount of light and air during the greater period of its growth. Starting as a seedling, the young tree struggles for many years in the cold and gloom of the underbrush, the first decade of its existence being merely a struggle for survival. This is evident from the figures in Table IV, in which so many trees show that over 30 years were passed in attaining their first inch of radius or two inches of diameter. Only through the survival of the fittest do these nurslings struggle upward until by overtopping the surrounding growth they gain light and air, after which their increase in rapidity of growth is plainly noticeable.

Now the black spruce of the Adirondacks does not require any such number of years to attain a merchantable size. On Lot 94, Township 21, in the Town of Long Lake, Hamilton county, there is at the present time a thick growth of spruce on a piece of land where the Rev. Robert Shaw, a local clergyman, according to his statement, mowed grass 26 years ago. Many of the trees in this clump of spruce are over 30 feet high and nine inches in diameter. Emerson* mentions seven spruce trees of 31 years' growth, in the Botanic garden, which averaged 30 inches in diameter, or one-third of an inch annual growth in diameter.

* Trees and shrubs of Massachusetts, by George B. Emerson.

In the office of the Forest Commission there are some carbon paper impressions showing growth rings taken from the stumps of spruce trees recently cut by lumbermen — trees which were growing in a spruce forest that had been lumbered 24 years ago, at which time all the larger spruce was taken out. The accelerated growth of the young spruces which were left, due to the admission of light and air through the removal of the large trees, is plainly seen in the wider rings shown by the carbon impressions taken from the stumps. Up to and just preceding the time when the lumbermen first went into this forest these spruces were growing at a rate of 26 rings to the inch. Immediately after this thinning and interlucation there was an increased growth, as shown by the impression paper, at the rate of 11 rings to two inches.

We regret exceedingly that we are unable to reproduce in print these impression papers of tree rings so as to furnish them with this publication, for they argue plainly and incontestably as to the increased product and revenue which can be derived from our spruce forests where the cutting is done under an intelligent system.

That the number of rings disclosed by the cross-section of a tree-trunk indicates the years of age is a generally accepted fact. It is so taught in all text-books pertaining to the subject. Asa Gray states that "the trunk of an exogenous tree, when cut off at the base, exhibits as many concentric rings of wood as it is years old."

Emerson* says of these tree rings that "a single circle attains maturity, in temperate regions, every year."

Goodale† states that this "development of the film of growth is usually continuous in a given season, but it may be interrupted, in which case it is possible to have two rings added to the wood in a single year, whereas, *as everyone knows, there is usually only one new ring for each year's growth.*"

The "interrupted" growth just referred to is the result of a period of cold weather acting upon trees which in the same season have felt previously the influence of an early spring. But in

---

* Trees and shrubs of Massachusetts, by George B. Emerson.

† Garden and Forest, Vol. II, March 20, 1889: Principles of Physiological Botany, as applied to Forestry; by George Lincoln Goodale.

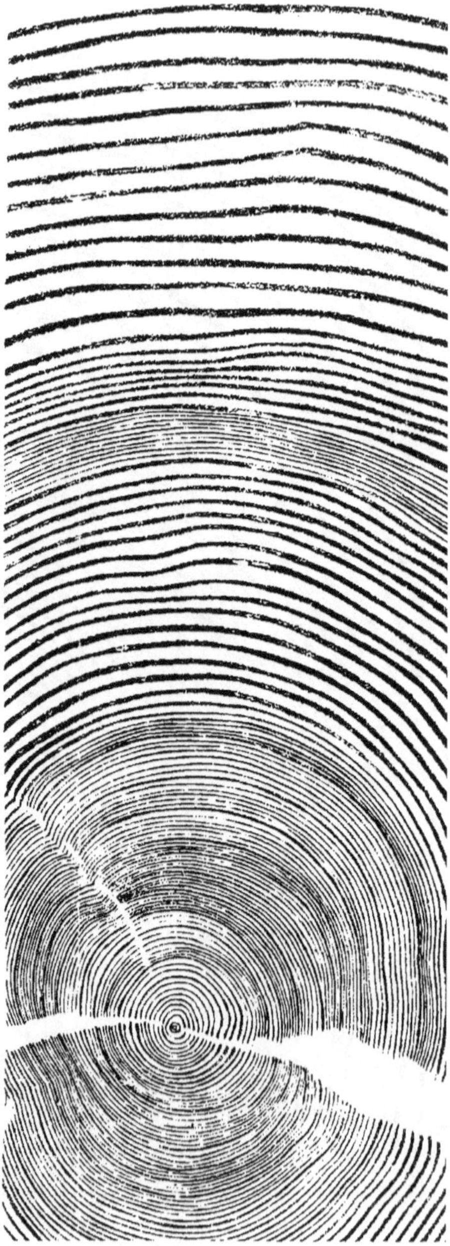

Cross-section of Black Spruce, 115 years old, 12 inches in diameter on the stump. From an impression made with carbon paper. The greater thickness of the outer rings is due to interlucation made by lumbermen eighteen years ago.

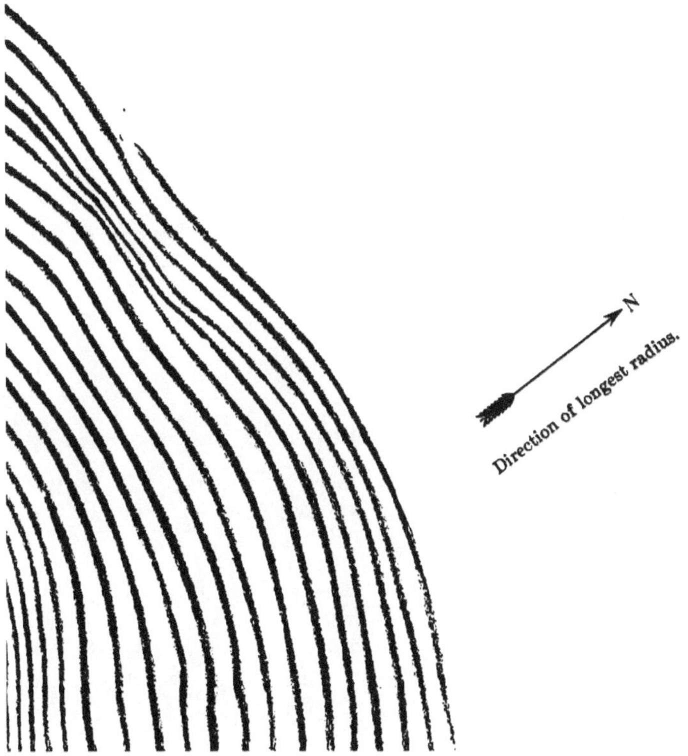

the cold, backward climate which prevails in the habitat of the Adirondack spruce there is no early spring, and no premature starting of the sap or liability to such interruptions. In that region spring is late in coming, and barely ushers in the summer.

Hough * says: "The record of the seasons for a long period may be determined, at least in effect, by the width of the rings of annual growth. We sometimes find, at recurring intervals, a narrow ring, perhaps every third year, that may have been caused by the loss of leaves from worms that appear at that interval, and that have thus left their record when every other proof of their presence has perished. We have seen sections of trees in the museums of Schools of Forestry, in which these proofs were recorded through a century or more of time, and the years could be definitely fixed by counting inward from the year when the tree was felled.

"When the bark and wood of a tree are cut or wounded by accident, as by the marking hammer of the forester, or the axe of a surveyor, the growth from the side will gradually close over the injury, and fill in the inequalities, so that, when afterward split off, it will often show in relief any depressions or cuts on the original trunk. Many Forest Academies in Europe have in their museums specimens of timbermarks thus cut or stamped into wood, with the cast taken by nature from the mold. The landmarks of surveyors have thus been found more than a hundred years afterward. Some scar, or, in coniferous trees, perhaps a gum spot, would be noticed upon the outside, and by cutting down through as many rings of growth as there had been years since the former survey, the marks of the ax would be found."

It is no new idea. Over 400 years ago, Leonardo da Vinci†, who was an observant botanist as well as a great painter, wrote: "The rings of the branches of trees show how many years they have lived, and their greater or smaller size whether they were damper or drier. They also show the direction in which they were turned, because they are larger on the north side than on the south, and for this reason the center of the tree is nearer the bark on the south than on the north side."

But these statements need not rest upon any botanical theory. In the course of our work we have often found it necessary to

---

* Elements of Forestry, by Franklin B. Hough, Ph. D.

† *Il Nuovo Giornale Botanico Italiano*: Vol. I, No. 1, 1869.

re-establish the old boundary lines of various townships in the Adirondack forest. The surveyors have repeatedly cut blocks out of line trees in which the old original "blaze" was grown over with wood and hidden from sight; but the number of tree rings outside the original but concealed scar of the blaze mark corresponded exactly with the number of years which had elapsed since the time when the surveyors first ran the line. This curious and interestiug phenomenon has been observed so often in the course of our work that it has ceased to attract attention as a novelty. Many suits involving the title to or possession of land have been decided in courts on the evidence of some surveyor who proved the date of an old survey by introducing as evidence a block of wood cut from a line tree.

In view of the general belief that the annular grains of tree growth are coincident in number with the years of age, it is interesting to note that this idea is strongly combated by some careful observers. While we do not agree with the conclusions in the following article, it is reproduced here as an interesting contribution to the literature pertaining to this subject. The article is reprinted from the *Saw-Mill Gazette :*

GROWTH RINGS ON TREES.

Age said not to be indicated by them.

"There is an old landmark on the DeLarm farm that is of considerable interest. The farm is located on what is known as the 'high road' to DuBois from Reynoldsville. The landmark, which is a notch in a tree, locates a corner of the DeLarm farm, which is in Jefferson county. The landmark also locates the boundary line between Jefferson and Clearfield counties. When the notch was cut Clearfield and Jefferson counties had not been organized, and the line ran between two other counties. The line still remains, though it does not now mark the boundary of either of the original counties. The notch was cut into the tree in 1785, just 108 years ago. This fact is proven by the rings in the tree that are visible and which number 108. Sometimes parts of a tree containing a notch similar to this one, establishing a corner, are taken into court and are accepted as evidence. The date, designated by the number of rings, is also accepted."—*Reynoldsville Volunteer*, Pa.

"The above item is from a recent copy of a Pennsylvania journal, and serves to show how tenaciously man clings to old fallacies. Of all silly notions this idea of rings being an indicator of the age of trees seems to be most sens-less, and yet, according to the above authority, the rings of a tree are accepted as evidence in courts.

If the determining of the age of a tree by the rings was one of those things that was difficult to controvert, then there might be some excuse for depending upon them, but when there are so many opportunities at hand to disprove the theory, to adhere to the fallacy is worse than ignorance—it becomes a species of bigotry.

Just how the notch proves what is asserted is not made clear, as any cut into the side of a healthy tree is sure to fill up by the outer growths after a series of years, but somewhere the authority for the statement found 108 rings, and forsooth the notch was cut 108 years ago; logic, and as a matter of course, "a horse chestnut must be a chestnut horse."

Had a section from an opposite side of the tree been cut there would have been found, without doubt, another number of rings, either less or more, or had the count been several feet above the notch the number would have been less, or below it a short distance there would have been found a greater number.

If the believers in the rings are to tell us the age of a tree thereby, they must settle just at what point the count is to be made for beginning at the ground and going upwards, it is found that the number of rings grows less as you ascend. This must be so from the natural course of things, as new shoots put out from the top and continue the upward growth of the tree every year. We can see no way out unless we make our count at the ground, but here even we encounter another difficulty, and one that is serious, if the tree should be one that has grown where one side is fully exposed to the sun and the other shaded. In that case, counting from the heart, it will be found that on the exposed side of the tree the number of rings is greatly in excess of the number on the shaded side.

A notable case is called to mind of a second-growth white ash that grew in a hedge on the south side of a fence. This tree showed forty clearly defined rings upon the south side of the heart, and, by a liberal allowance, after examining with a magnifying glass, thirty was the most that could be defined on the north side, so that it was just as easy to prove the tree thirty as it was to prove it forty years old. The same butt was cut off eight feet above the cutting kerf, and the number of rings had been reduced to twenty and sixteen. Curiosity led to a further examination and the stump was cut close to the ground, where no difficulty was experienced in counting sixty and forty-five rings, respectively.

A further proof was furnished by the recorded facts of the fence having been erected on that line thirty-five years before, as a boundary line between the estates of two brothers, being a part of a plot that was divided up between heirs, and the tree grew after the fence was built. Of course, such a case would not count against the prejudice of ages, but it becomes a stubborn fact, nevertheless.

Let anyone plant a number of seed — apple, peach or plum, something that grows quickly — care for the sprouts, and after three or four years cut them and count the growth-rings and thus satisfy himself. It is doubtful if two out of a dozen will contain the same number of rings, or if anyone will show a number corresponding with the age. The thriftier the shoot the greater the number of rings, and the more stunted and weak the specimen the less the number, and yet all may be of the same age and grown under similar conditions.

All roots, those used for food as well as those that are not, are of a woody nature, and where the circumstances are unfavorable the least thrifty of the edible show a fibrous, woody composition, and at times some are found that can not be cooked to make them fit for food. In all the growth rings are defined, but in none so clearly as in the beet. Not only does it show the rings, but it shows the porous state and medullary rays as well. These rings neither indicate days, months, moons or other time divisions. On a tender, thrifty root there may be a dozen or more rings, while a less thrifty one grown at its side may not show half that number. What will our seer tell us regarding the ages of these beets?

Leaving all other tests aside, there is a law of nature that upsets all this annular ring growth theory. Everything has its growing, ripening and decaying season. The tree, like the straw of wheat, grows to its full, ripens and then dies. A tree may be vigorous and put on wood, or, in other words, grow for one hundred years, but that hundred years does not mark its life; for fifty or even a hundred more years the life sap may be sufficient to nourish and maintain the growth already made, but not enough to put on new wood, and another fifty or hundred years may pass, during which no new growth is made, and during which the vital fluid is sufficient to maintain the tree in full vigor, during which it slowly but surely dies. Here may be three hundred years of life, and yet, during two hundred years, not an ounce of new wood has been added, and yet, in face of all, men will assert that they can determine the age of a tree by its rings.

What, then, are these rings and what do they determine? The common-sense answer is, they are growth rings — nothing more. One may be the result of a year, a month or a week or any other division of time; all depends upon circumstances. If an entire summer has been moist and vegetation has suffered no drawback from drouth or cold, it is barely possible that the entire growth of that season will be represented by a single ring, but even this is doubtful, as it is the thin sap which flows nearest the bark that nourishes the growth, and if an extra large growth is formed the sugar and glutinous matter in the sap may thicken and impede the flow of the more watery portion, and by forcing it into the new inner bark cause a new growth; but if, after a growing period, there comes a drouth sufficient to rob the roots of the necessary moisture, the sap in the wood thickens and the more watery seeks the inner bark, through which it carries nourishment to the leaves. This is often insufficient, and many leaves fall and others wilt, but with a fall of rain the supply of vital fluid is increased, the leaves brighten up and the smaller ones grow. New life is imparted, and with this new life comes a new growth, another ring is formed, and so on through the entire season Who living in the north has not seen the leaves nipped by a frost after they were full and fall to the ground? After a few warm days and a warm rain new leaves start and the tree is soon in full foliage, but there has been a check to growth and a new growth starts with the new leaf. Thus, one cause another checks one growth and invites another, making a ring each time entirely independent of years."—*Saw-Mill Gazette.*

Mr. Austin Cary, of Bangor, Me., who, acting under instructions from the National Forestry Bureau, has been engaged in the Maine forests in counting tree rings with a view to establishing the age of the black spruce in that State, calls attention in his report to certain facts which throw some light on this matter of variable or retarded tree growth:

"While carrying out the field work, which is behind all these statements, facts were found proving the influence of the weather on the growth of trees. In May, 1893, while at work on the Androscoggin river, word came from Mr. J. A. Pike, of Berlin, N. H., that record was to be seen in the spruces of a series of cold years which occurred in the early part of the century. This was richly worth examination, and I immediately set about investigating the matter. Beginning the count of rings with the bark, it was found on the first log examined that a number of rings, being in that case the seventy-ninth to the eighty-third from the bark, were very distinctly thinned. Continuing the search, every tree was found to have a belt of thin rings in substantially the same position, these being reduced in some cases almost to microscopic.

"As soon as access could be had to books the history of the matter was looked up, and it was found that the years 1812 to 1816 in Maine were very extraordinary years. The temperature was unusually low as an average, and in 1812, 1815 and 1816, at least, frosts or snows or both occurred in the summer. In 1815 and 1816 crops through the State were very seriously impaired, and many people despairing of the agricultural prospects of the

G. H. Rison, Photo.

LOG HAULING IN THE ADIRONDACKS.

(At the "double-header.")

country emigrated to the Ohio valley. This severe weather then was without doubt the cause of the thin rings so regularly found in the spruce trees.

" Since that time this zone of rings has been found in spruce trees in all parts of the State and in the northern portion of New Hampshire. Careful notes of its character and occurrence were taken, in the course of other study, and the facts observed and inferences drawn will be found in full in the publications of the United States Forestry Division.

"This belt of thin rings can be seen by anyone who will take the trouble to examine carefully any good sized spruce log. It demonstrates the effect of inclement seasons on the growth of trees, and it is further of value in that while there is some variation about it, the approximate regularity of its position, the close correspondence in number of the rings outside the thin belt with the seasons that have elapsed since the cold year, gives added confidence in the substantial regularity of ring deposit and consequently in the results of investigation which proceed on that assumption.

" An instance of the effect o. exposure on the growth of trees I am able to present through the interest of Mr. William Monroe, of Bangor. In the winter of 1893-94 he scaled* a landing of spruce hauled into Silver lake in the Town of Katahdin Iron Works, from a piece of ground on the south slopes of Saddle Rock Mountain, which had never before been cut. The soil was a deep red loam, and the spruce was gathered along brook runs or scattered amongst the hardwood growth intervening. But the point is that the timber was divided between two separate slopes of the mountain, the upper one of which was some 200 feet above the lower, and considerably more exposed.

"The timber from each slope was yarded on the more level land at its base, and Mr. Monroe kept a separate scale of the two lots. A marked difference in the size of the trees is found. The logs cut on the upper and more exposed slope were 4,377 in number, and scaled 435,726 feet, B. M., or 99½ feet to the piece. The lower lot numbered 2,598 sticks, and the total scale was 320,811 feet, or 123½ feet to the piece. The difference is 24 per

* Measured.

cent. of the smaller piece. No other cause for it being apparent, the difference in the size of the trees seems to be due to their greater or less exposure."

FOREST COMPOSITION.

Throughout the entire forest, covering the Adirondack Plateau, where the altitude exceeds 1,300 feet, the hardwood growth accompanying the black spruce is in almost every locality made up of maple, beech and yellow birch. Here and there, but at widely separated intervals, are scattering specimens of the white and black ash, black cherry, elm, basswood, "hard-hack"* (*Ostrya Virginica*), and white birch. On burned areas or reforested clearings the poplars and "pin" cherries (*Prunus Pennsylvanica*) grow in abundance, but are seldom seen growing with the spruce in the primeval woods.

In order to give some idea of the general composition of the Adirondack woods, the foresters were directed to measure off in different places an acre or more of ground and count each tree within the space, noting, also, its diameter and species. They were further instructed to take pains that the localities selected should be ones in which the growth had no unusual characteristics, and which would fairly represent the number and proportion of the various species per acre.

Foresters Olmstead and Sanford accordingly selected four acres on Lot 39, Township 20, Franklin county, in the immediate vicinity of the forest in which they examined the trees embraced in the first 700 specimens of Table IV. These four acres are situated about four miles west of the head of the Upper Saranac Lake, and near the line of the Adirondack division of the New York Central railroad. Their notes do not embrace the young trees of seven inches in diameter or less, of which there was the usual proportion standing among the others. The undergrowth, like that of all the Adirondack forests, was somewhat dense, being composed largely of "witch hopple" (*Viburnum lantanoides*) and striped maple (*Acer Pennsylvanicum*). The mountain maple (*Acer spicatum*) was not plentiful, this species apparently seeking the roadsides or openings.

* Local, for iron-wood.

TABLE VII.

Acre No. 1.

Lot 39, *Township* 20, *Franklin County.*

Diameter.	Spruce.	Hemlock.	Balsam.	Birch.	Maple.	Beech.	
8 inches	20	8	2	......	1	22	53
9 "	6	5	1	......	......	7	19
10 "	8	2	2	1	4	13	30
11 "	4	1	.....	......	1	5	11
12 "	4	4	1	1	8	11	29
13 "	7	......	......	......	3	3	13
14 "	1	......	......	2	2	3	8
15 "	......	......	......	2	......	......	2
16 "	......	......	......	2	5	4	11
17 "	......	......	......	......	......	......	.....
18 "	......	......	......	......	2	2	4
19 "	......	......	......	......	......	......	.....
20 "	1	1	......	3	4	......	9
21 "	......	......	......	......	......	......	.....
22 "	......	......	......	......	1	......	1
23 "	......	......	......	......	......	......	.....
24 "	......	1	......	1	......	......	2
25 "	......	......	......	......	......	......	.....
26 "	......	......	......	......	......	......	.....
27 "	......	......	......	......	......	......	.....
28 "	......	......	......	1	......	......	1
	51	22	6	13	31	70	193

Average diameter, including eight inches and upwards: — Spruce, 10 inches; hemlock, 10½ inches; balsam, 9½ inches; yellow birch, 17¼ inches; maple, 14⅕ inches; beech, 10½ inches.

TABLE VIII.

Acre No. 2.

Lot 39, *Township* 20, *Franklin County.*

Diameter.	Spruce.	Hemlock.	Balsam.	Birch.	Maple.	Beech.	Total.
8 inches	18	13	5	1		16	53
9 "	3	3	2			2	10
10 "	7	4		3		8	22
11 "	6	2			2	2	12
12 "	5	11	1	3	1	10	31
13 "	5	2		3			10
14 "	3	3		2	3	1	12
15 "	1						1
16 "	1	1			2	1	5
17 "	1				1		2
18 "	3			1			4
19 "							
20 "				2			2
	53	39	8	15	9	40	164

Average diameter, including eight inches: Black spruce, $10\frac{4}{5}$ inches; hemlock, $10\frac{3}{8}$ inches; balsam, $8\frac{3}{4}$ inches; yellow birch, $13\frac{1}{4}$ inches; hard maple, $13\frac{5}{9}$ inches; beech, $9\frac{9}{10}$ inches.

TABLE IX.

Acre No. 3.

Lot 39, *Township* 20, *Franklin County.*

Diameter.	Spruce.	Hemlock.	Balsam.	Birch.	Maple.	Beech.	Total.
8 inches	18	15	2	1	.....	25	61
9 "	6	....	......	......	......	......	6
10 "	17	10	......	2	1	10	40
11 "	5	2	1	......	......	3	11
12 "	14	6	......	8	2	6	36
13 "	6	....	......	1	......	......	7
14 "	11	2	......	3	1	3	20
15 "	1	1	......	2	......	......	4
16 "	2	....	......	2	......	3	7
17 "	......	....	......	1	......	......	1
18 "	......	1	......	2	2	......	5
19 "	......	....	......	......	......	......	.....
20 "	......	....	......	......	......	......	.....
21 "	1	....	......	......	......	......	1
22 "	1	1	.....	......	1	......	3
23 "	......	....	......	......	......	......	.....
24 "	1	2	......	.....	2	......	5
29 "	......	1	......	......	......	......	1
33 "	......	1	......	......	......	......	1
	83	42	3	22	9	50	209

Average diameter, including eight inches: Black spruce, $11\frac{3}{4}$ inches; hemlock, $12\frac{1}{4}$ inches; balsam, 9 inches; yellow birch, $13\frac{1}{3}$ inches; hard maple, $17\frac{1}{9}$ inches; beech, $9\frac{4}{5}$ inches.

TABLE X.

Acre No. 4.

Lot 39, *Township* 20, *Franklin County.*

Diameter.	Spruce.	Hemlock.	Balsam.	Birch.	Maple.	Beech.	Total.
8 inches	14	9	1	1	......	5	30
9 "	......	......	......	......	......	......	.....
10 "	9	4	1	1	......	5	20
11 "	5	......	......	......	......	2	7
12 "	11	4	......	4	1	5	25
13 "	4	......	......	1	......	......	5
14 "	6	2	......	1	......	4	13
15 "	3	......	......	1	2	2	8
16 "	......	......	......	3	1	4	8
17 "	2	......	......	......	......	......	2
18 "	4	......	......	......	1	......	5
19 "	......	......	......	......	......	......	.....
20 "	......	......	......	2	1	.....	3
21 "	1	......	......	......	1	......	2
22 "	1	......	......	......	......	......	1
23 "	......	......	......	......	......	......	.....
24 "	......	......	......	......	......	1	1
28 "	......	1	......	......	......	......	1
33 "	......	1	......	......	......	......	1
	60	21	2	14	7	28	132

Average diameter, including eight inches: Black spruce, $11\frac{9}{10}$ inches; hemlock, $11\frac{6}{7}$ inches; balsam, 9 inches; yellow birch, 14 inches; hard maple, $16\frac{5}{7}$ inches; beech, $12\frac{1}{3}$ inches.

The trees noted in the next table were counted and measured by Foresters Olmstead and Sanford on an acre located on Lot 31, Township 19, Town of Altamont, Franklin county. On this acre all trees above four inches in diameter were included in the forester's notes. Although in a different township and several miles to the westward it will be noticed that the composition of this piece of forest is essentially the same as that shown in the four preceding tables.

TABLE XI.

ACRE No. 5.

Lot 31, *Township* 19, *Franklin County.*

DIAMETER.	Spruce.	Hemlock.	Balsam.	Birch.	Maple.	Beech.	Total.
5 inches	21	1	13	......	1	1	37
6 "	7	3	6	1	......	2	19
7 "	7	2	4	......	......	1	14
8 "	15	1	12	......	1	14	43
9 "	......	......	......	......	......	......	.....
10 "	13	2	......	3	......	5	23
11 "	2	1	......	......	......	2	5
12 "	9	4	2	1	2	15	33
13 "	......	1	......	......	......	4	5
14 "	3	4	......	1	1	3	12
15 "	......	1	......	......	......	1	2
16 "	11	4	......	4	2	2	23
17 "	......	......	......	......	......	......	.....
18 "	8	2	......	......	......	1	11
19 "	......	......	......	1	......	......	1
20 "	......	......	......	2	......	......	2
21 "	......	1	......	......	......	......	1
22 "	3	......	......	......	1	......	4
23 "	......	......	......	......	......	......	.....
24 "	2	......	......	1	1	......	4
	101	27	37	14	9	51	239

Average diameter, including five inches: Black spruce, $10\frac{4}{10}$ inches; hemlock, $12\frac{1}{5}$ inches; balsam, $6\frac{3}{4}$ inches; yellow birch, $14\frac{9}{10}$ inches; hard maple, $14\frac{1}{3}$ inches; beech, $10\frac{3}{5}$ inches.

The general composition of the Adirondack forest is fairly represented by the species shown in the five preceding tables. But in traveling through the wilderness exceptional forest tracts will be often noted. In some localities, as shown in Table XII, the hemlock predominates, and the spruce is of secondary importance. In others the white pine, which has nearly disappeared from the Adirondacks, is still to be found. Then, again, in some places only one of the three dominant hardwoods is growing.

In illustration of these exceptional types of timber land we furnish here some tables based on notes and measurements made by Forester Frank C. Parker, who was instructed to examine certain tracts in Essex county.

TABLE XII.

Acre No. 1.

Lot No. 12, *Roaring Brook Tract, Essex County, N. Y.*

SPECIES.	Trees.	Diameters in inches.	Standards *	Feet, B. M.	Cords.
Black Spruce (*Picea nigra*)	11	12—16	6.90	1,262	2
Hemlock (*Tsuga Canadensis*)................	35	12—40	92.00	16,836	.....
Yellow Birch (*Betula lutea*)	6	8 - 30	......	......	.....
Hard Maple (*Acer saccharinum*)..................	5	19—28	......	......	.....
Beech (*Fagus ferruginea*).	36	10—24	......	......	.....
Basswood (*Tilia Americana*)............. ...	1	20—	......	......	.....
Totals	94	......	98.90	18,098	2

Notes.—This acre was selected in a virgin forest, situated on a gentle slope, well watered, with an easterly exposure. Ground slightly rolling. A fair type of forest in which the hemlock predominates. The altitude is about 1,700 feet. The land is owned by the State.

TABLE XIII.

Acre No. 2.

Lot No. 12, *Roaring Brook Tract, Essex County, N. Y.*

SPECIES.	Trees.	Diameters in inches.	Standards.	Feet, B. M.
Black Spruce (*Picea nigra*)......	11	8—17	4.55	832
Hemlock (*Tsuga Canadensis*)....	7	16—28	12.08	2,210
Balsam (*Abies balsamea*)........	10	7—16	2.96	541
White Cedar (*Thuya occidentalis*)	13	10—20	9.13	1,671
Yellow Birch (*Betula lutea*)......	38	10—21	......	....
Beech (*Fagus ferruginea*).......	7	12—20	......	....
Totals	86	......	28.72	5,254

Notes.—On high land with an easterly exposure. The surrounding forest has the appearance of having been burned over at some previous time, many years ago. The original field-notes pertaining to the survey of this lot call for a corner on a burned hill. This corner is only a short distance from the strip on which these measurements were made. The hardwood has the appearance of a second growth, and some of the larger ones show the effects of fire.

* A "standard" log is 13 feet long and 19 inches in diameter at the smallest end, inside the bark, and contains 183 feet of lumber, board measure. In the Adirondack forests the lumbermen cut all their logs 13 feet long.

TABLE XIV.

Acre No. 3.

Lot No. 12, *Roaring Brook Tract, Essex County, N. Y.*

SPECIES.	Trees.	Diameters in inches.	Standards.	Feet, B. M.	Cords.
Black Spruce (*Picea nigra*).	28	8—21	21.54	3,942	6
Hard Maple (*Acer saccharinum*)	47	10—28	......	......	.....
Beech (*Fagus ferruginea*).	43	7—21	......	......	.....
Totals	118	......	21.54	3,942	6

Notes.—This acre is a primitive forest in which the hardwoods predominate. It is on a piece of table land, well watered from slopes on either side. The maples and beeches are thrifty and tall, this acre being a good type of an Adirondack forest in which there is a good growth of spruce intermixed among the hardwoods. The undergrowth is composed largely of Mountain Maple (*Acer spicatum*) and small Yellow Birch.

TABLE XV.

Acre No. 4.

Lot No. 12, *Roaring Brook Tract, Essex County, N. Y.*

SPECIES.	Trees.	Diameters in inches.	Standards.	Feet, B. M.	Cords.
Black Spruce (*Picea nigra*).	73	9—18	37.00	6,771	12
Hemlock (*Tsuga Canadensis*)	3	12—30	9.98	1,826	.....
White Cedar (*Thuya occidentalis*)	46	9—22	18.24	3,338	.....
White Pine (*Pinus strobus*).	12	24—37	101.55	18,583	.....
White Birch (*Betula papyracea*)	11	8—16	......	......	.....
Totals	145	......	166.77	30,518	12

Notes—This acre represents a portion of virgin forest situated on rising ground, well watered, a small brook running through a portion of it. The slope has a westerly exposure. It is a fair example of the ridges on which the spruce predominates, and where it grows in company with other conifers.

TABLE XVI.

ACRE No. 5.

Lot No. 12, Roaring Brook Tract, Essex County, N. Y.

SPECIES.	Trees.	Diameters in inches.	Standards.	Feet, B. M.	Cords.
Black Spruce (*Picea nigra*).	36	9—20	15.49	2,834	4
Hemlock (*Tsuga Canadensis*)................	40	8—26	17.37	3,178	.....
White Cedar (*Thuya occidentalis*)..............	6	9—26	6.60	1,208	.....
Hard Maple (*Acer saccharinum*)...............	12	11—28	......	......	.....
Beech (*Fagus ferruginea*).	43	6—19	......	......	.....
White Ash (*Fraxinus Americana*)...........	1	20—	......	......	.....
Totals................	138	......	39.46	7,220	4

NOTES.—This acre was selected in a primitive forest, growing on a "bench" or natural terrace, well watered, with a northerly exposure. The undergrowth, in addition to the nurslings of the dominant species, was composed largely of Mountain Maple (*Acer spicatum*), with occasional specimens of Striped Maple (*Acer Pennsylvanicum*). The growth under and near the hemlocks was completely covered in places with the American Yew or Ground Hemlock (*Taxus Canadensis*).

TABLE XVII.

ACRE No. 1.

Lot No. 206, Township 11, O. M. Tract, Essex County, N. Y.

SPECIES.	Trees.	Diameters in inches.	Standards.	Feet, B. M.	Cords.
Black Spruce (*Picea nigra*).	52	5—16	14.49	2,651	4
Hemlock (*Tsuga Canadensis*)................	26	9—28	20.00	3,660	.....
Balsam (*Abies balsamea*)..	44	7—16	9.00	1,647	.....
Yellow Birch (*Betula lutea*)	37	6—20	......	......	.....
Hard Maple (*Acer saccharinum*)...............	14	8—22	......	......	.....
Totals................	173	......	43.49	7,958	4

NOTES.—This lot (206, Township 11) was lumbered about 33 years ago by C. F. Norton, at which time the pine and spruce were cut; but the spruces under 10 inches in diameter were not taken. Since then—about 16 years ago—it was cut over again, at which time some white ash and yellow birch was taken, as well as the larger spruce.

This acre strip was measured off on level land, not low enough to be swampy, but a bench of table land. The crown covering is dense; and the timber, with the exception of the hemlock and some of the hardwoods, seems to be a second growth,—that is, it has been growing among first-growth trees, and has made a rapid progress after the interlucation made by cutting out he larger trees.

TABLE XVIII.

ACRE NO. 2.

Lot No. 206, *Township* 11, *O. M. Tract, Essex County, N. Y.*

SPECIES.	Trees.	Diameters in inches.	Standards	Feet, B. M.	Cords.
Black Spruce (*Picea nigra*)	51	5—16	20.00	3,660	7
Hemlock (*Tsuga Canadensis*)	15	10—24	24.00	4,392	.....
Balsam (*Abies balsamea*)	38	7 -16	10.00	1,830	.....
Tamarack (*Larix Americana*)	5	7—12	......	......	.....
Yellow Birch (*Betula lutea*)	30	10—23	......	......	.....
Soft Maple (*Acer dasycarpum*)	14	8—20	......	......	.....
Totals	153	......	54.00	9,882	7

NOTES.—This acre was measured off at the extreme end of a bench of table land extending toward a swamp. The undergrowth is mostly small yellow birches and mountain maples, the latter appearing only where the cutting had been severe, evidently places where the ground was originally cleared for skidways.

TABLE XIX.

ACRE NO. 3.

Lot 206, *Township* 11, *O. M. Tract, Essex County, N. Y.*

SPECIES.	Trees.	Diameters in inches.	Standards	Feet, B. M.	Cords.
Black Spruce (*Picea nigra*)	15	8—22	9.00	1,647	3
Balsam (*Abies balsamea*)	5	7—14	.....	.....	....
Hard Maple (*Acer saccharinum*)	30	9—28	.....	.....	.....
Beech (*Fagus ferruginea*)	39	7—20	.....	.....	.....
Totals	89	.....	9 00	1,647	5

NOTES.—This acre was selected on a hardwood slope with a northerly exposure. Interspersed with the larger trees there was a large number of small yellow birches and maples, and in places, groups of small balsams, all under five inches in diameter. Only a few of the hardwood trees had been cut by the lumbermen.

The crown development was dense, and the forest in good condition.

TABLE XX.

Acre No. 4.

Lot 206, *Township* 11, *O. M. Tract, Essex County, N. Y.*

Species.	Trees.	Diameters in inches.	Standards.	Feet, B. M.	Cords.
Black Spruce (*Picea nigra*).	36	8–22	15	2,745	5
Hemlock (*Tsuga Canadensis*)	30	12–27	20	3,660	.....
Balsam (*Abies balsamea*) ..	10	6–12	......	......	.....
Yellow Birch (*Betula lutea*)	27	7–24	......	......	.....
Beech (*Fagus ferruginea*).	40	8–20	......	......	.....
Black Cherry (*Prunus serotina*)	3	6–20	......	......	....
Totals	146	....	35	6,405	5

Notes.—This acre is on land sloping toward the east On this strip there is a cluster of spruces that have all the appearances of being a "first-growth," although the trees are not large. It is evident that at the time of the first cutting these trees were considered too small for saw logs.

In several instances the owners of spruce timber lands in northern New York have shown an encouraging and commendable tendency to manage their property with reference to sustained productivity. Instead of taking all the merchantable timber available for immediate profit, they have restricted their cutting materially with the intention of securing further growth and further revenues in future. The cutting of small spruces for pulpwood has been prohibited on many large tracts, although the revenue derivable from this source is large and available at any time. Furthermore, the cutting for lumber or saw-logs is restricted to trees 12 inches in diameter on the stump.

Although this is a step in the right direction, and something of an improvement on previous methods, there is little in it worthy of the name of forestry. As an approach to scientific or even intelligent forestry methods it is a very slight advance indeed.

It is true that spruce lands in our State have been cut over a second and even a third time, at intervals of 25 years or thereabout, and that such cuttings have proved remunerative. But this was not rendered possible altogether by any increase in the

G. H. Rison, Photo.

LUMBER CAMP.
(Roof covered with spruce bark.)

rate of growth due to the interlucation resulting from a previous thinning of the trees; nor in any great degree to the natural increase in size during the intervals.

These successive crops of spruce were due for the most part to other reasons. In the first cutting only the larger and easily accessible trees were taken. Large trees were often left because it did not pay to cut roads to them, the roads being confined to the areas on which the timber grew thickly. In the second cutting roads were extended into these areas of scattered spruces, some slight increase in market price warranting this additional expense. The large trees left at the first cutting were then taken out, together with many others which had become large enough through this additional period of growth. The third cutting becomes feasible 25 years later by reason of increased market values, improved means of access, and the demand for pulpwood — the latter demand alone making it profitable in many instances to cut over an old tract where the sawing timber by itself would not yield enough to pay the expense of "lumbering" it. Of course, the younger spruces increase in size during the intervals between operations, and at each return the axeman finds some trees large enough for saw-logs which previously were too small. But too much stress has been laid on this factor in the question, while too many other and important points have been ignored.

Assuming that our spruce forests are to be managed, for a period at least, under the well-recognized and accepted forestry method known as that of "selection," we will waive the all-important question of cutting for improvement, and turn to that of cutting for revenue — for future and continuous revenue as some of our well-intentioned forest owners are pleased to term it.

This method, which for convenience may be termed cutting for revenue, can not secure the desired result — that of the perpetual maintenance of a merchantable species — unless the cutting is confined to mature trees only. Nothing short of this will answer. Now, it would be difficult to say just what diameter should be assumed in defining a matured spruce. This is evident from the figures in the preceding tables. Moreover, this diameter must vary in different localities. Such diameter can not be ascertained, if at all, until working plans covering a century of improvement cutting, seeding or planting have been exploited. It would be idle to discuss it here.

But if there is to be no improvement cutting, if our forest owners prefer to start with a fixed diameter as a basis for restriction in revenue cutting — "a rule of thumb," as Dr. Fernow calls it — such diameter can be fixed approximately in each locality; and when thus determined, if it approximates closely the average diameter of the matured spruce, it may answer as a first step in a right direction. Such diameter need not be fixed at the maximum. On the contrary, something should be subtracted to offset what is termed in forestry the interest account. A perfectly managed forest is one that will produce the greatest possible revenue and maintain it. It is evident that as a tree approaches maturity there comes a time in its slowly waning growth after which the increment will not equal in value the interest on the money obtainable if cut at that time. Before felling a tree it is not necessary to wait for the signs of decay that announce the cessation of growth. The tree may be turned into money before that, and, in view of the interest account, thus yield a greater profit than to wait for its maximum development.

It would be impossible to name any diameters here which should govern such cutting. But any owner of spruce lands can arrive approximately at the proper size if the question is approached intelligently and honestly. Certainly, the twelve inch limit now in use falls far below such requirements. A tree sixteen inches in diameter yields twice as much lumber as one of twelve inches; and one twenty inches yields four times as much.

By harvesting matured trees only, the land owner receives the legitimate income from his property, and makes it a perpetual, interest-bearing investment; by harvesting the timber before it attains its growth, he decreases the future productivity of his land, and, for the sake of immediate returns, makes a heavy draft upon the principal. Moreover, if he confines his cutting for revenue to mature trees he not only preserves his principal intact, but by adding to his work some judicious improvement cutting he can increase the value of the principal and its corresponding productivity.

Many owners of spruce lands have been encouraged by the repeated crops attainable from cutting on a basis of ten or twelve inches in diameter on the stump to assume that such returns may be obtained perpetually. Even if this could be done the yield

G. H. Rison, Photo.

DRIVING LOGS.

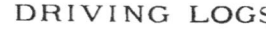

thus obtained must be inferior in quantity and value, like any crop that is gathered before it is ripe or has attained its full growth.

It is maintained by experienced foresters, and with good reason, that the persistent cutting of any one species, especially where it is done before the trees have attained their full size, tends to the deterioration and, ultimately, to the extinction of such species. This ought to be evident without going into the technical reasons.

It is not intended in this report to criticise unfavorably the land owners who are willing to accept pay for twelve-inch spruce. It is their property, and if they prefer the cash in hand to future payment they have the right to accept it without comment. In fact, many who advocate other methods would probably do the same if they were fortunate enough to own spruce timber lands. But the owners of woodlands who are able to hold them, and who may wish to manage their forest so that it will yield the greatest revenue, and are willing to waive immediate returns in favor of a permanent, revenue producing investment will do well to study this question carefully.

The felling of immature spruce merely for revenue should be discontinued. Mature trees, however, should be converted into money. Part of this money could be set aside with advantage as a fund from which to pay the expense of improvement cuttings, through which the growth of desirable species would be fostered and inferior ones eliminated. The work of the axeman should not be limited to the mature trees which are cut for revenue, but should include the removal of all diseased trees and inferior species, large and small, even though such timber does not yield one cent to pay for the work. Then, again, it might be necessary often to allow sound, mature trees to remain, because their removal might influence surrounding conditions so unfavorably as to inflict a loss greater than their value. But to go further into this subject would involve the recital of technical details of management which are foreign to the scope of this article.

Some mention should be made here of the natural tendency of the Adirondack spruce to reproduce itself, a fortunate characteristic that, under the guidance of skillful foresters, could be utilized with great advantage in the work of forest improvement. But land owners who persist in cutting down to a small diameter on the stump should not rely on this natural seeding of the spruce to correct their faulty system. In the dissemination of spruce seed and starting of natural plantations, nature has proved whimsicals and while the young spruces generally succeed the poplars and bird cherries on the burned lands, they often fail to restock the lands of their own habitat which have been rendered bare by injudicious cutting.

The thrifty landowner who would manage his spruce lands rightly should not only confine his cutting to sound methods, but should employ a skillful forester whose judicious, fostering care of the seedlings, together with some provision for the dissemination of seed, will insure that future stability of income which is the main object and aim of intelligent, scientific forestry.

The foregoing paragraphs have dealt solely with the question of the black spruce, because the other merchantable species in the Adirondack forests growing in company with it are seldom accessible. The white pine, except in few localities, was removed years ago. The hemlock is valuable mainly on account of its bark, and in many townships is not cut at all. The hardwoods, though merchantable near the borders of the forest, owing to their accessibility, are not marketable for the most part, as the logs can not be floated down the streams.

Still, the roads and railways which are penetrating the forest in increased numbers are fast rendering the hardwoods accessible. The time is near when most of the broad-leaved trees in the Adirondacks, as well as the conifers, will become merchantable species. The same provisions which should regulate the cutting of the spruce will apply to them also. The value and productivity of these timber lands will be correspondingly increased, and with the proper management of our woodlands American forestry will occupy its rightful place as a beneficent factor in our political economy.

www.ingramcontent.com/pod-product-compliance
Lightning Source LLC
Chambersburg PA
CBHW021943160426
43195CB00011B/1200
* 9 7 8 3 3 3 7 1 7 7 3 1 7 *